T0322215

Jane's Patisserie

EVERYDAY

Jane's Patisserie

EVERYDAY

EASY CAKES AND COMFORT BAKES

JANE DUNN

EBURY
PRESS

Contents

Introduction

Hey, I'm Jane Dunn and I'm back with another book of utterly delicious recipes that you are going to want to devour. I'm a food-obsessed baker, cook, blogger and author of all things yummy and I hope you enjoy these recipes as much as I enjoyed creating them.

I have loved baking and cooking since I was little, so much so I went to cookery school to train to be a chef and it was the best thing that I could have done. It gave me the confidence to understand flavours, the chemistry behind baking and it was the spark that I needed to pursue my love of food as a career. I started my blog on a whim because I wanted to continue exploring my passion by creating my own recipes and I was amazed by the amount of people that started following along. It wasn't just my parents and my friends supporting me, it was people all over the world, millions of people wanting to bake and share my recipes with their friends and family too.

The fact that my blog has brought me to bake live on stage (something I could never *ever* have imagined when I was younger) and also live on national television is unbelievable. I want to say a BIG thank you to my followers for their support from the very beginning: without you I wouldn't be on this journey, and I can't thank you enough for helping me grow my love and passion for food into the thing I now do every day!

If my journey has taught me anything it's that a love of food is something that everyone can relate to. We all have our favourite sweet treat or comfort dish that we reach for to give us a happy boost, or a go-to bake to share with friends, and my goal has always been to create recipes that anyone can make no matter what their skill level might be. You don't need to be an expert to enjoy baking and you don't need a kitchen full of the latest equipment to put delicious treats on the table, and that's exactly what this book is about: delicious easy bakes that you can enjoy every day.

I've been saving up all the best recipe requests from my wonderful followers and this book is FULL of brand-new goodies – say hello to my decadent **Brownie Cake** (page 24), gooey **Coconut NYC Cookies** (page 57), my easy no-bake **Passion Fruit Cheesecake** (page 121) and lots more. I've also included popular classics from my blog – like my retro

Chocolate School Cake and Custard (page 173), my delicious **Salted Caramel Pretzel Cupcakes** (page 35) and my moreish **Honeycomb Fudge** (page 234).

As well as the usual sections for all your favourite sweet treats, I've also worked in more savoury dishes too. In **Tarts, Pies and Pastries**, you'll find yummy summery fruit combos as well as cosy quiches and crunchy filo-topped pies, in **Comfort Food** you'll find warming crumbles, one-tray feasts and simple savoury dinners like my gooey **Macaroni Cheese** (page 146) and in **Savoury and Breads** you'll find winning snacks and sides like my **Loaded Potato Skins** (page 197) or my **Camembert Tear and Share Bread** (page 204) – perfect for a night in with friends or for when you just fancy a bit of a picky tea! In **Free-From Every Day** I've included my top tips on how to make many of my recipes suitable for a vegan or gluten-free diet, and a few vegan and gluten-free recipes too – so there really is something for everyone.

I wanted to make sure that the recipes in this book were accessible but, most of all, I tried to fill it with the kind of dishes that you will come back to over and over again. I hope this book brings you all as much joy and love as it has me.

Ingredients

Most of your cupboards will be full of the baking basics, but here is a simple list of ingredients needed for the bakes in this book:

- **Flours** – self-raising, plain, strong white bread
- **Sugars** – caster, icing, soft light brown, soft dark brown, granulated
- **Dairy** – butter, baking spread, cheeses, milk, cream
- **Eggs** – I use medium size
- **Dry ingredients** – cornflour, cocoa powder, dried yeast, baking powder, bicarbonate of soda, instant coffee
- Baking colourings and flavourings
- **Storecupboard** – pasta, rice, passata, oils, pulses
- A spice selection
- Salt and pepper
- **Chocolates** – 70% dark, milk, white
- Dried fruits and nuts
- Jams, spreads, condensed milk, tinned caramel
- Cake decorations
- Fresh vegetables
- Fresh meats
- Fresh fruits

Equipment

There are certain pieces of equipment that I recommend all of the time for my recipes, so here is a rough list. You don't need all of them to achieve great results, but it might make your baking life just a little bit easier:

- Weighing scales
- Large baking trays
- Oven thermometers
- Mixing bowls
- Spatulas and whisks
- Measuring spoons
- Timer
- Sieve
- Frying pan
- Round pan
- Small and large piping bags
- Piping nozzles
- Cookie scoops
- Rolling pin
- Stand mixer
- Food processor
- **Cake tins** – 20cm round, 23cm square, 23cm tart tin, 23 x 33cm traybake tin, 900g loaf tin
- 12-hole muffin tray
- Trifle and dessert bowls
- Baking dish
- Roasting tray
- Cookie cutter set

Freezing

The general rule for me and freezing is that basically anything can be frozen. I never want to waste a thing!

1. RAW COOKIE DOUGH CAN BE FROZEN FOR 3+ MONTHS.
   - Add 2 minutes to the baking time.

2. FROZEN BAKED GOODS CAN BE KEPT FOR 3+ MONTHS.
   - Wrap cakes in a double layer of cling film and then foil.
   - All other baked goods, such as brownies, cookies and desserts, will need to be sealed in a freezer-safe container.
   - Defrost in the fridge if it needs to stay chilled once thawed, such as a cheesecake, or defrost on the kitchen side if it is stored at room temperature normally.

3. SAVOURY DISHES AND SNACKS CAN BE PREPPED AND FROZEN BEFORE COOKING AND KEPT FOR 3+ MONTHS.
   - Increase the cooking time by 5-10 minutes.

4. SAVOURY DISHES AND SNACKS CAN BE FROZEN, AFTER COOKING AND COOLING, AND KEPT FOR 3+ MONTHS.
   - Reheat by defrosting in the fridge overnight or in the morning of the day they are needed, and then reheat generally 160°c 180°c, until piping hot.

Top Tips

All recipes have full instructions, and even some useful notes – but here are some handy top tips that help with any recipe!

1. BE ACCURATE

Inaccurate measuring of ingredients can cause so many problems! Weighing scales or measuring spoons are vital.

2. PREHEAT THE OVEN BEFORE BAKING

The temperature makes a difference. Sometimes oven thermometers can also save you as ovens can vary SO MUCH.

3. HAVE PATIENCE

I know it's annoying, but a cheesecake needs the time to set, and you don't want to decorate a warm cake.

4. READ THROUGH THE RECIPE

Know in advance what you have to do so there are no surprises.

5. KNOW YOUR EQUIPMENT

New equipment can change how a recipe turns out, so sometimes practice makes perfect.

6. EXACT INGREDIENTS

Make sure that you use the correct ingredients. Lower-fat versions or alternatives can change or even ruin a recipe completely. Switching flavours or decoration can work however, see my swap suggestions in the recipe notes for ideas and inspiration.

7. HAVE FUN!

I know this sounds silly but try not to worry and just have fun.

Cakes and Cupcakes

MILLIONAIRE'S CAKE

This cake has always been insanely popular since I shared it on my blog. Whenever the photo is posted on social media it goes crazy, but how can it not?! Taking the classic flavours of Millionaire's Shortbread and reimagining it as three layers of brown sugar sponge, topped with chocolate buttercream, gooey caramel and shortbread bites, oh my days, it really is DELICIOUS.

SERVES: 15+

PREP: 30 minutes
BAKE: 25–30 minutes
COOL: 2 hours
DECORATE: 20 minutes
LASTS: 3+ days,
at room temperature

400g unsalted butter, at room
    temperature
400g soft light brown sugar
400g self-raising flour
7 eggs

Buttercream

350g unsalted butter, at room
    temperature
650g icing sugar
75g cocoa powder

Decoration

350g ready-made caramel sauce
15 shortbread bites
50g shortbread
Sprinkles

Preheat the oven to 180°C/160°C fan and line three 20cm deep cake tins with parchment paper.

In a large bowl, beat the butter and sugar together for a few minutes until light and fluffy.

Add the flour and eggs and beat again briefly until combined. Divide the mixture between the three tins and smooth it over.

Bake for 25–30 minutes until the cakes are golden and the cake springs back when you press it with your finger. (A skewer inserted into the middle should also come out clean.) Leave the cakes to cool in their tins for 10 minutes or so, then remove and leave to cool fully on a wire rack.

Buttercream

In a large bowl, beat the butter for a few minutes to loosen it. Add the icing sugar and cocoa powder and beat again until smooth. If it is really thick, add 1 tablespoon of boiling water at a time, beating well each time, until smooth and combined.

Decoration

Place the first cooled sponge onto the serving plate and pipe a third of the buttercream onto the cake. Spread or drizzle a third of the caramel onto the buttercream. Repeat with the second sponge. Top with the third sponge and decorate with the remaining buttercream. Drizzle over the last of the caramel.

Add a shortbread bite to each slice, and sprinkle over some crushed shortbread biscuits and some sprinkles.

NOTES

- *You can make chocolate sponges by substituting 75g of the self-raising flour for cocoa powder, and chocolate caramel buttercream by adding 75g caramel sauce to it.*

RED VELVET CAKE

This blog favourite Red Velvet Cake is so incredibly moreish. You can find red velvet cake all over the place, but it can be easy to get wrong. This modern version uses extra strong food colouring to get the iconic bold red colour (avoid supermarket own brands as they do not work as well), and the rise comes from a mix of buttermilk, bicarbonate of soda and vinegar. The soft cheese frosting just finishes it off perfectly.

SERVES: 15

PREP: 30 minutes
BAKE: 30–35 minutes
COOL: 2 hours
DECORATE: 20 minutes
LASTS: 3+ days,
in the fridge

125g unsalted butter, at room temperature
300g caster sugar
3 eggs
30g cocoa powder
1 heaped tsp extra strong red food colouring
1 tsp vanilla extract
250ml buttermilk
300g plain flour
1 tsp bicarbonate of soda
2 tsp white wine vinegar

Frosting
150g unsalted butter, at room temperature
150g icing sugar
300g full-fat soft cheese
1 tsp vanilla extract

Preheat the oven to 170°C/150°C fan and grease and line two 20cm deep cake tins.

In a large bowl, cream the butter and sugar together until smooth and fluffy, then add the eggs, cocoa powder, food colouring and vanilla extract. Add the buttermilk, flour, bicarbonate of soda and vinegar and beat until smooth and combined.

Divide the mixture between the two tins and bake in the oven for 30–35 minutes until a skewer inserted into the middle of the cakes comes out clean. Leave to cool fully on a wire rack. Once cool, level the cakes slightly if you wish (keep the offcuts as you can use these for decoration).

Frosting

In a large bowl, beat the butter for a few minutes to loosen it. Add the icing sugar and beat again for about 5 minutes. Take the soft cheese and drain off any excess water – I find it best to add it to a bowl first, just to make sure. Beat the soft cheese and vanilla extract into the butter and icing sugar mixture. At first, it may look a little weird, but continue to beat until the lumps disappear and the frosting is smooth and thick.

Pipe or spread half of the frosting on top of one sponge. Top with the other sponge, then pipe or spread the remaining frosting on the top and decorate with sponge crumbs if you fancy.

NOTES

- It's so important to measure the ingredients accurately for the sponge as the rise, colour and flavour depend on it.

- Make sure that you use really good-quality food colouring so that the cake turns red.

- You MUST use full-fat soft cheese for the frosting, otherwise it may turn out runny.

LEMON DRIZZLE BUNDT CAKE

This crowd-pleasing lemon drizzle is an everyday bake taken to the next level simply by baking it in a beautiful bundt tin. Lemon drizzle is always popular – moist and packed full of flavour, it's a great option to make for friends or a celebration as it doesn't need too much faffy decoration, but it still has a special impact.

SERVES: 12

PREP: 20 minutes
BAKE: 65–70 minutes
COOL: 2 hours
DECORATE: 15 minutes
LASTS: 4+ days,
at room temperature

300g unsalted butter, at room temperature, plus extra melted, for greasing
300g caster sugar
6 eggs
300g self-raising flour, plus extra for dusting
Zest of 3 lemons

Drizzle
75ml lemon juice
75g caster sugar

Decoration
100g icing sugar
1–2 tbsp lemon juice
Lemon zest

Preheat the oven to 160°C/140°C fan and very generously grease and flour a 9–10-cup (2.5-litre) bundt tin with melted butter and flour.

In a large bowl, beat the butter and sugar until light and fluffy. Add the eggs, flour and lemon zest and beat again until combined. Pour this mixture into the tin and bake for 65–70 minutes.

Drizzle
While the cake is baking, put the lemon juice and caster sugar into a pan and dissolve the sugar over a low heat. Let the mixture cool while the cake bakes.

Once the cake has baked, poke a few holes in the sponge and pour the drizzle over. Leave to soak in for 15–20 minutes, then turn the cake out onto a wire rack to cool completely.

Decoration
Mix the icing sugar and lemon juice together until you have a thick paste. Drizzle the icing over the cake. Sprinkle on some lemon zest for decoration.

NOTES
- Using a bundt is one of the easiest ways to produce a showstopping cake, but you have to make sure that you really prep the tin perfectly. I brush or spray the tin with butter or oil spray and generously douse it in flour before gently tapping out excess.

PINEAPPLE
UPSIDE DOWN CAKE

This iconic and nostalgic bake is so incredibly easy to make. It only needs one tin and can be ready to enjoy in just over an hour, so is great for any last-minute gatherings or when you just need to satisfy those sweet cravings FAST. A simple cake mixture, baked on top of pineapple rings and glacé cherries, topped with a sugar glaze, I love mine with a smothering of custard, but my mum's favourite is ice cream.

SERVES: 6–8

PREP: 20 minutes
BAKE: 40–45 minutes
COOL: 2 hours
LASTS: 3+ days,
at room temperature

Fruit topping

50g unsalted butter, at room
  temperature
65g soft light brown sugar
7 tinned pineapple rings, drained
  and syrup reserved
7 glacé cherries (optional)

Cake

150g unsalted butter, at room
  temperature
150g caster sugar
150g self-raising flour
3 eggs
1 tsp vanilla extract

Preheat the oven to 180°C/160°C fan.

To make the fruit topping, beat the butter and sugar together until creamy. Spread this mixture onto the bottom of a 20cm deep cake tin. Arrange the pineapple rings on the sugar mixture and place a cherry inside each one.

In large bowl, beat the butter and sugar together until light and fluffy. Add the flour, eggs and vanilla extract and beat until combined. Pour this mixture over the pineapples and cherries and spread until even.

Bake in the oven for 40–45 minutes. Leave the cake to cool in the tin for 10 minutes, then carefully remove by turning out onto a plate. Brush the top of the cake with any leftover pineapple syrup from the tin if you fancy.

NOTES

- Take this to the next level by making it into a two-layer cake – just double the recipe and bake in two 20cm tins. Sandwich with a sweetened cream made from 150ml double cream, 2 tablespoons of icing sugar and ½ teaspoon of vanilla extract whipped together.

- The glacé cherries are optional, but they look good and add a little extra sweetness.

BROWNIE CAKE

As you may have realised through following my recipes, I love a mash-up.
My Carrot Cake Cheesecake on page 114, my Bronuts on page 216, and this beauty
– a brownie turned into a layered cake for the ultimate luxury bake. You get the gooey,
fudgy and luxurious brownie texture sandwiched with a deliciously easy
buttercream. Everyday meets showstopper. What could be better?!

SERVES: 15

PREP: 30 minutes
BAKE: 20–23 minutes
COOL: 3 hours
DECORATE: 30 minutes
LASTS: 3+ days,
at room temperature

300g dark chocolate
300g unsalted butter
400g soft light brown sugar
6 eggs
150g plain flour
75g cocoa powder
100g dark chocolate chips
100g milk chocolate chips
100g white chocolate chips

Decoration

250g unsalted butter, at room
   temperature
500g icing sugar
1 tsp vanilla extract
Chocolate sprinkles
Chocolate chips

Preheat the oven to 180°C/160°C fan and line two 20cm cake tins with parchment paper.

In a heatproof bowl, break up the dark chocolate into pieces and add the butter. Melt together in the microwave in shorts bursts or set the bowl over a pan of simmering water (bain-marie) until smooth. Leave to cool for 10 minutes.

In a new bowl, whisk the sugar and eggs together for a few minutes until the mixture has become mousse-like and the whisk leaves a trail in the mixture. Pour in the melted chocolate mixture and fold together gently. Pour in the flour and cocoa powder and fold together gently until combined. Finally, fold in all the chocolate chips.

Split the mixture between the two tins. Bake the brownies in the oven for 20–23 minutes, or until there is still a slight wobble in the middle of the tins. Leave to cool fully in the tins. Then chill in the fridge for 2 hours to create a fudgy texture.

Decoration

Beat the butter for a minute or two to loosen. Add the icing sugar and vanilla extract and beat until smooth. Transfer to a piping bag with the piping nozzle of your choice fitted and pipe most of the buttercream onto one brownie. Place the second brownie on top. Pipe the last of the buttercream over the top layer, and decorate with sprinkles and some chocolate chips.

NOTES

- *It's so important to use dark chocolate with at least 70% cocoa content to get the best results for the brownie base, but you can use whatever chocolate chips you want.*

- *You can flavour this brownie cake really easily with peppermint extract, orange extract, almond extract, coffee extract etc… 1–2 teaspoons works perfectly.*

HUMMINGBIRD CAKE

If you haven't heard of hummingbird cake, you are missing out. It's a banana, pineapple, spiced nutty sponge, sandwiched with soft cheese frosting – and it's a little out of this world. It's the sort of cake that everyone will want an extra slice of, and I don't blame them. This beauty has three layers of heaven, perfect for sharing with friends and family.

SERVES: 15

PREP: 30 minutes
BAKE: 30–35 minutes
COOL: 2 hours
DECORATE: 30 minutes
LASTS: 3+ days,
in the fridge

350g self-raising flour
1 tsp ground cinnamon
½ tsp ground nutmeg
170ml vegetable oil/sunflower oil
350g soft light brown sugar
4 eggs
5 ripe bananas, mashed
400g pineapple chunks
150g pecans, chopped

Frosting

250g unsalted butter, at room
  temperature
250g icing sugar
500g full-fat soft cheese
1 tsp vanilla extract

Decoration

100g pecans, chopped

Preheat the oven to 180°C/160°C fan and line three 20cm deep cake tins with parchment paper.

In a large bowl, beat the flour, cinnamon, nutmeg, oil, sugar and eggs together until smooth. Add the mashed bananas, pineapple chunks and pecans and fold together until smooth.

Divide the mixture between the three tins and bake in the oven for 30–35 minutes, or until baked through. Leave to cool in the tins for 30 minutes, then remove to a wire rack to cool completely.

Frosting

In a large bowl, beat the butter for a few minutes to loosen it. Beat in the icing sugar for about 5 minutes. Take the soft cheese and drain off any excess water – I find it best to add it to a bowl first, just to make sure. Beat the soft cheese and vanilla extract into the butter and icing sugar mixture. At first, it may look a little weird, but continue to beat until the lumps disappear and the frosting is smooth and thick.

Decoration

Add the first sponge to a plate and spread or pipe on a third of the frosting. Repeat with the second layer, then the third. Sprinkle some chopped pecans over the top.

NOTES

- *This classic bake should feature all of the ingredients for best results, but if you can't eat nuts, then leave them out, or swap the pecans for a different nut such as walnuts or hazelnuts if you prefer.*

- *Make sure you use full-fat soft cheese for the frosting for best results.*

CHOCOLATE ORANGE FUDGE CAKE

Oh I know, I know, I know... another chocolate orange bake?! Well, I simply had to. This is such a highly requested recipe and one of the cakes I have wanted to share with you all for ages. Delicious, super-fudgy chocolate sponges flavoured with orange, sandwiched with the best chocolate orange frosting you will ever make – and decorated with as much orange and chocolate orange-flavoured bits you can get, of course. An easy, perfect bake to indulge in at the weekend.

SERVES: 15

PREP: 30 minutes
BAKE: 40–45 minutes
COOL: 2 hours
DECORATE: 30 minutes
LASTS: 3+ days,
at room temperature

225g dark chocolate
225g unsalted butter
1 tbsp instant coffee
125ml boiling water
175g plain flour
25g cocoa powder
1 tsp baking powder
¼ tsp bicarbonate of soda
400g soft light brown sugar
Zest of 2 large oranges
4 eggs
75ml buttermilk

Frosting
250g unsalted butter, at room
    temperature
500g icing sugar
1 tsp orange extract
75ml evaporated milk
1 tsp orange food colouring
50g cocoa powder

Preheat the oven to 160°C/140°C fan and line two 20cm deep cake tins with parchment paper.

In a heatproof bowl, break up the dark chocolate into pieces and add the butter. Melt together in the microwave in shorts bursts or set the bowl over a pan of simmering water (bain-marie) until smooth.

Dissolve the instant coffee in the boiling water and mix together. Add the coffee mix to the chocolate/butter mix and stir well until smooth.

In a separate large bowl, add the flour, cocoa powder, baking powder, bicarbonate of soda, sugar and orange zest and mix well. In a separate bowl, mix the eggs with the buttermilk.

Add the chocolate mixture and egg mixture to the dry ingredients and stir together, trying not to overmix – it should be thick but runny with no floury lumps. Split the mixture between the two tins and bake in the oven for 40–45 minutes. Leave to cool fully in the tins.

Frosting
In a large bowl, beat the butter for several minutes until smooth and supple. Add the icing sugar and beat until combined. Add the orange extract and evaporated milk and beat again. Take a third of the frosting and mix in the orange food colouring. Add the cocoa powder to the other two-thirds and mix.

Decoration

150g orange marmalade
Orange slices
Orange zest
Chocolate orange segments

Decoration

Place a cooled sponge on a serving plate and spread the orange frosting on top.

Spread the marmalade on top of the orange frosting. Add the second sponge and slather the chocolate orange frosting over the top and sides of the cake. Decorate with orange slices, orange zest and chocolate orange segments.

NOTES

- *You can make your own buttermilk by adding 1 teaspoon of lemon juice to 75ml whole milk. Let it sit for 5 minutes before using.*

- *Once the instant coffee has dissolved and been added to the cake mix, you can't taste it, but it enhances the flavour of chocolate, so please still use it even if you don't like coffee.*

CHOCOLATE HAZELNUT LOAF CAKE

This deliciously easy loaf cake with a swirl of chocolate hazelnut spread baked through, a whipped chocolate hazelnut frosting and a sprinkling of decoration is so easy to throw together and you only need one tin. I love loaf cakes because they're so simple to make – you only need to slather something on the top and you're done! I've made this one so many times for my family and friends and it always disappears within minutes – a guaranteed crowd-pleaser.

SERVES: 8

PREP: 20 minutes
BAKE: 55–60 minutes
COOL: 1 hour
DECORATE: 10 minutes
LASTS: 3+ days,
at room temperature

250g unsalted butter, at room
  temperature
250g soft light brown sugar
5 eggs
250g self-raising flour
150g chocolate hazelnut spread
  (I use Nutella)

Decoration

150g chocolate hazelnut spread,
  plus 50g melted
75ml double cream
8 chocolate hazelnut sweets (I use
  Ferrero Rocher)
50g chopped hazelnuts

Preheat the oven to 180°C/160°C fan and line a 900g loaf tin with parchment paper.

In a large bowl, beat the butter and sugar until light and creamy. Add the eggs and flour and beat again until smooth. Melt the chocolate hazelnut spread slightly in a pan over a very low heat, or in a heatproof bowl in the microwave until runny.

Pour two-thirds of the cake mixture into the tin, then pour over the melted chocolate hazelnut spread, and swirl slightly. Pour over the remaining cake mixture. Bake the cake in the oven for 55–60 minutes, or until baked through. Leave to cool fully in the tin.

Decoration

Add the chocolate hazelnut spread to a bowl with the double cream and whip together until soft peaks form. Spread or pipe the mixture over the top of the cooled cake, then drizzle on the melted chocolate hazelnut spread. Arrange one chocolate hazelnut sweet per slice and sprinkle over the chopped hazelnuts.

NOTES

- *If you want to make a buttercream to go with this cake instead, beat 100g unsalted butter with 200g icing sugar, then beat in 100g chocolate hazelnut spread.*

- *You can swap the chocolate hazelnut spread for a non-nutty spread or any other spread you fancy.*

SALTED CARAMEL PRETZEL CUPCAKES

These utterly scrumptious blog favourites marry so many of my own favourite things. Salted pretzels are pretty much my downfall – I could eat a bag within minutes – so adding them into a bake is an absolute game changer. A blended pretzel base topped with a cupcake sponge, a salted caramel buttercream, finished with more caramel and topped off with a pretzel make these impressive treats perfect for a party.

MAKES: 12
PREP: 30 minutes
BAKE: 18–22 minutes
COOL: 1 hour
DECORATE: 30 minutes
LASTS: 3+ days,
at room temperature

100g salted pretzels
150g unsalted butter, at room temperature, plus 35g melted
150g soft light brown sugar
150g self-raising flour
3 eggs

Buttercream

100g salted caramel sauce
150g unsalted butter, at room temperature
300g icing sugar

Decoration

100g salted caramel sauce, plus extra for drizzling
Pretzels

Preheat the oven to 180°C/160°C fan and get 12 cupcake cases ready on a baking tray.

Blitz or crush the pretzels to a fine crumb and mix in the melted butter. Divide between the 12 cases and press down firmly.

In a large bowl, beat the butter and sugar together until light and fluffy. Add the flour and eggs and beat again until smooth. Divide between the 12 cases and bake in the oven for 18–22 minutes. Leave to cool fully on a wire rack.

Buttercream / Decoration

Core out the centre of the cupcakes and fill with salted caramel sauce.

Beat the butter for a couple of minutes to soften it. Add the icing sugar and beat again until combined. Add the salted caramel sauce and mix until smooth. Transfer to a piping bag with the piping nozzle of your choice fitted and pipe the buttercream onto the cupcakes. Drizzle with extra salted caramel sauce. Sprinkle over some crushed pretzels and add a whole pretzel to each cupcake.

NOTES

- *You can use a regular caramel sauce if you don't like salted caramel, or you can add salt to a regular caramel (see my recipe on page 77) to make your own salted caramel.*

- *If you can't find salted pretzels (or don't have time to shop), you can make a mixture of blended biscuits for a biscuit base – try 100g digestive biscuits and 35g melted butter instead.*

IRISH COFFEE CUPCAKES

We can all appreciate the idea of an Irish coffee, right? Even if you aren't so keen on the drink, in a cupcake it's just something else. These cupcakes are perfectly moist and light, but still packed so full of flavour. An easy bake that you could make on any day, but also just a little bit special, so great for a last-minute celebration.

MAKES: 12

PREP: 30 minutes
BAKE: 20–22 minutes
COOL: 1 hour
DECORATE: 30 minutes
LASTS: 3+ days,
at room temperature

2 tbsp instant coffee
2 tbsp boiling water
175g unsalted butter
175g soft light brown sugar
1 tsp vanilla extract
3 eggs
175g self-raising flour
100ml Irish cream liqueur
  (I use Baileys Original)

Decoration

200g unsalted butter, at room
  temperature
400g icing sugar
75ml Irish cream liqueur
Chocolate curls

Preheat the oven to 180°C/160°C fan and get 12 cupcake cases ready on a baking tray.

Add the instant coffee and boiling water to a cup and dissolve the coffee. Let it cool for 5 minutes.

In a bowl, beat the butter and sugar until combined. Add the vanilla extract, eggs and flour and beat again. Pour in the cooled coffee, the Irish cream liqueur and mix again until smooth.

Divide the mixture between the 12 cases and bake in the oven for 20–22 minutes. Leave to cool fully on a wire rack.

Decoration

Beat the butter for several minutes to smooth and loosen it. Add the icing sugar and beat again. Gradually add the Irish cream liqueur, beating as you go, until light and fluffy.

Transfer to a piping bag with the piping nozzle of your choice fitted and pipe the buttercream onto the cupcakes with your favourite piping tip. Sprinkle over some chocolate curls.

NOTES

- I use a classic Irish cream liqueur, but you can use a flavoured one, or any cream-based liqueur.

- Make the cupcakes chocolate flavoured by swapping 35g of the flour for cocoa powder in the sponge mix, or the buttercream, or both!

MINT CHOCOLATE CUPCAKES

I am an absolute obsessive when it comes to the classic chocolate and mint flavour combination – it is so delicious, and I will just eat it over and over (basically every day). These cupcakes have a mint chocolate sponge, filled with a mint water icing for a gooey centre, topped with a chocolatey-mint buttercream... and, you guessed it, more chocolate mint. Some would say they are a little OTT, but me? I say they are DELICIOUS!

MAKES: 12

PREP: 30 minutes
BAKE: 20–22 minutes
COOL: 1 hour
DECORATE: 30 minutes
LASTS: 3+ days,
at room temperature

150g unsalted butter, at room
    temperature
150g soft light brown sugar
125g self-raising flour
25g cocoa powder
3 eggs
1 tsp peppermint extract (optional)

Filling

150g icing sugar
1 tsp peppermint extract
2–3 tsp water

Buttercream / Decoration

200g unsalted butter, at room
    temperature
335g icing sugar
65g cocoa powder
1 tsp peppermint extract (optional)
12 mint chocolates (I use After
Eight)

Preheat the oven to 180°C/160°C fan and get 12 cupcake cases ready on a baking tray.

In a large bowl, beat the butter and sugar together until light and fluffy. Add the flour, cocoa powder, eggs and peppermint extract, if using, and beat again until smooth.

Divide the mixture between the 12 cases and bake in the oven for 20–22 minutes. Leave to cool fully on a wire rack.

Filling

Once the cupcakes have cooled, core out the middles with a small knife, or you can use a piping tip by pushing it in slightly, twisting and lifting it out.

In a small bowl, slowly mix the icing sugar with the peppermint extract and water until you have a thick paste. Fill the holes with the mint icing.

Buttercream / Decoration

In a large bowl, beat the butter for a few minutes to loosen it. Add the icing sugar and cocoa powder and beat again. Add the peppermint extract if you'd like to use it. If the buttercream is really thick, add boiling water, 1 tablespoon at a time, beating really well until combined and smooth. Transfer to a piping bag with the piping nozzle of your choice fitted and pipe the buttercream onto the cupcakes, sealing in the peppermint centres. Decorate with some mint chocolates.

NOTES

- *This bake works well with other flavours – try swapping the mint to orange, almond, coffee, lemon or anything you fancy.*

CARAMEL PECAN CUPCAKES

I love the pairing of caramel and nuts – it's a heavenly sweet and slightly savoury combination and I would eat it every single day if I could. When I was asked over and over to make a caramel pecan cupcake, I simply had to oblige. A deliciously nutty cupcake sponge, topped with a caramel sauce with a little salt, and even more pecan caramel goodness on top – what could be better than that?

MAKES: 12

PREP: 30 minutes
BAKE: 20–22 minutes
COOL: 1 hour
DECORATE: 30 minutes
LASTS: 3+ days,
at room temperature

150g unsalted butter, at room
temperature
150g soft dark brown sugar
150g self-raising flour
3 eggs
1 tsp vanilla extract
150g pecans, chopped

Buttercream

175g unsalted butter, at room
temperature
350g icing sugar
75g caramel sauce (see page 77)
Pinch of sea salt (optional)

Decoration

50g caramel sauce
50g pecans, chopped
Sprinkles

Preheat the oven to 180°C/160°C fan and get 12 cupcake cases ready on a baking tray.

In a large bowl, beat the butter and sugar together until light and fluffy. Add the flour, eggs and vanilla extract and beat again until smooth. Fold through the chopped pecans. Divide the mixture between the 12 cases and bake in the oven for 20–22 minutes. Leave to cool fully on a wire rack.

Buttercream / Decoration

In a large bowl, beat the butter for a few minutes to loosen it. Add the icing sugar and beat again until combined. Add the caramel sauce and the salt, if using, and beat until you have a lovely smooth buttercream. Transfer to a piping bag with the piping nozzle of your choice fitted (I used a 2d closed star) and pipe the buttercream onto the cupcakes. Drizzle the caramel over the cupcakes and sprinkle on the chopped pecans and sprinkles.

NOTES

- Feel free to use any nut you want instead of the pecans.

- You can find the recipe for my caramel sauce on page 77 but shop-bought works perfectly too.

COCONUT
MANGO CUPCAKES

This is my best fruity cupcake yet. It's deliciously sweet and incredible on a summery day, or whenever you just fancy something sweet. A simple coconut cupcake, with a centre of mango purée, a mango buttercream frosting and a tasty decoration... DELIGHTFUL.

MAKES: 12

PREP: 30 minutes
BAKE: 18–22 minutes
COOL: 1 hour
DECORATE: 30 minutes
LASTS: 3+ days,
at room temperature

100g unsalted butter, at room
  temperature
125g caster sugar
150g self-raising flour
1 tsp baking powder
2 eggs
125ml coconut milk
40g desiccated coconut

Filling

225ml mango purée

Buttercream / Decoration

175g unsalted butter, at room
  temperature
350g icing sugar
60ml mango purée
100g mango chunks
25g coconut flakes

Preheat the oven to 180°C/160°C fan and get 12 cupcake cases ready on a baking tray.

In a large bowl, beat the butter and sugar together until light and fluffy. Add the flour, baking powder and eggs and beat again until smooth. Add the coconut milk gradually while mixing slowly, then fold through the desiccated coconut.

Divide the mixture between the 12 cases and bake the cupcakes in the oven for 18–22 minutes. Leave to cool fully on a wire rack.

Filling

Once the cupcakes have cooled, core out the middles and fill with the mango purée.

Buttercream / Decoration

In a large bowl, beat the butter for several minutes to loosen it. Add the icing sugar and beat until combined. Continue to mix while slowly adding the mango purée, so the buttercream remains thick.

Transfer to a piping bag with the piping nozzle of your choice fitted and top the cupcakes however you like. Decorate the cupcakes with some mango chunks and coconut flakes. The coconut flakes can be toasted in a dry frying pan over a medium heat, moving often, until beautiful and golden, if you like.

NOTES

- *You can make your own mango purée by blending mangoes, then pushing the mixture through a sieve to get the smooth texture you need. Or you can buy a shop-bought tin.*

- *It's very important to use unsalted butter when making this buttercream and not a spread or margarine of any kind as it will be too soft.*

CHOCOLATE CHEESECAKE MUFFINS

Muffins are one of those bakes that I think are slightly overlooked in favour of their cousins, the cupcake. I, however, LOVE them. Especially when they are stuffed with a baked cheesecake like these bad boys. These Chocolate Cheesecake Muffins have a chocolate-based muffin studded with chocolate chips, which is then filled and baked with a very easy vanilla cheesecake. Simple but showstopping.

MAKES: 12

PREP: 30 minutes
BAKE: 25–27 minutes
COOL: 1 hour
LASTS: 3+ days,
at room temperature

125g unsalted butter, at room
    temperature
150g soft light brown sugar
1 egg
1 tsp vanilla extract
175ml soured cream or natural
    yoghurt
½ tsp bicarbonate of soda
¼ tsp sea salt
50g cocoa powder
275g self-raising flour
175ml whole milk
250g milk chocolate chips

Cheesecake

250g full-fat soft cheese
100g caster sugar
1 egg
1 tsp vanilla extract

Topping

75g milk chocolate chips

Preheat the oven to 180°C/160°C fan and line a 12-hole muffin tray with tulip muffin cases.

In a large bowl, beat the butter and sugar together until light and fluffy. Add the egg, vanilla extract and soured cream and beat again until smooth. Add the bicarbonate of soda, sea salt, cocoa powder and flour to a separate bowl and whisk to combine. Add the dry ingredients to the butter mixture, along with the milk, and mix with a spatula until smooth. Fold through the chocolate chips.

Cheesecake

Add the soft cheese to a bowl and beat with a small spatula until smooth. Add the sugar, egg and vanilla extract and beat again gently until combined.

Assembly

Add a tablespoon of cake mixture to each muffin case, then add a spoonful of cheesecake mixture on top. Add another tablespoon of cake mixture and sprinkle over the extra chocolate chips. Bake in the oven for 25–27 minutes. Leave to cool fully on a wire rack.

NOTES

- *You can use dark or white chocolate chips instead of milk chocolate chips if you fancy, or even any chopped flavoured chocolate.*

- *If you want a plain muffin, you can leave out the cheesecake mixture.*

WHITE CHOCOLATE RASPBERRY MUFFINS

These fan favourites are an incredibly easy everyday bake, with the perfect level of sweetness, sharpness and flavour. The decoration is optional, so you can leave that out and make these even quicker if you're short on time.

MAKES: 12

PREP: 15 minutes
BAKE: 25–30 minutes
COOL: 1 hour
DECORATE: 10 minutes
LASTS: 3+ days,
at room temperature

160ml sunflower/vegetable oil
150ml whole milk
1 egg
1 tsp vanilla extract
300g self-raising flour
200g caster sugar
150g white chocolate chips or
  chopped chocolate
150g fresh raspberries

Decoration (optional)

75g white chocolate, melted
5g freeze-dried raspberries

Preheat the oven to 180°C/160°C fan and line a 12-hole muffin tray with cases.

In a bowl, whisk together the oil, milk, egg and vanilla extract. Add the flour and sugar and, using a spatula, mix together as little as possible until combined. Add the white chocolate chips and raspberries and fold through.

Divide the mixture evenly between the 12 cases and bake in the oven for 25–30 minutes. Leave to cool fully in the tray, or on a wire rack.

Decoration

Once cooled, drizzle over some melted white chocolate and sprinkle over some freeze-dried raspberries if you like.

NOTES

- *You can make other flavours of muffin by swapping the chocolate to milk chocolate, dark chocolate or any flavoured chocolate.*

- *Switch the raspberries for any other berry you fancy – I love using blueberries, and then adding in the zest of a lemon for a delicious muffin.*

Cookies and Traybakes

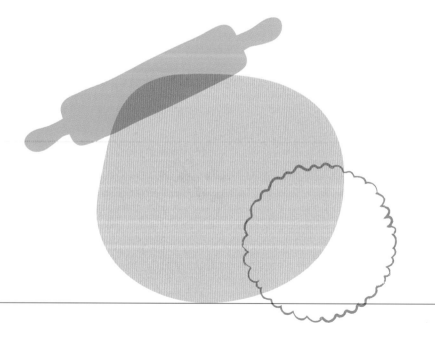

PEANUT BUTTER
NYC COOKIES

Peanut butter is one of those ingredients that has a cult following, so adding it to bakes is a simple way to elevate the everyday. These NYC-style cookies, which are giant, chunky and delicious, are one of the best things you can bake with peanut butter, and a blog favourite. The slight saltiness from the peanut butter combined with the sweetness of the white chocolate is the best marriage for a cookie.

MAKES: 8

PREP: 20 minutes
CHILL: 30+ minutes
BAKE: 11–12 minutes
COOL: 30 minutes
LASTS: 3+ days,
at room temperature

100g unsalted butter, at room
　temperature
100g crunchy or smooth peanut
　butter
100g soft light brown sugar
75g white granulated sugar
1 egg
1 tsp vanilla extract
275g plain flour
1 tbsp cornflour
1½ tsp baking powder
½ tsp bicarbonate of soda
½ tsp sea salt
150g white chocolate chips
100g peanut butter chips
100g peanuts, chopped

In a large bowl, beat the butter, peanut butter, light brown sugar and granulated sugar until creamy. Add the egg and vanilla extract and beat again. Add the flour, cornflour, baking powder, bicarbonate of soda and sea salt and beat until a cookie dough is formed. Add the white chocolate chips, peanut butter chips and peanuts and beat until well distributed.

Weigh the cookie dough and roll lightly into eight balls about 125g each. Chill in the freezer for at least 30 minutes, or in the fridge for an hour or so. While the cookies are chilling, preheat the oven to 200°C/180°C fan.

Take the cookies out of the freezer or fridge and divide between two large, lined baking trays. Bake in the oven for 11–12 minutes. Leave them to cool on the trays for at least 30 minutes, as they will continue to bake while cooling.

NOTES

- You can freeze the cookie dough before baking for 3+ months and bake the cookies whenever you want. Just add 1–2 minutes to the baking time.

- You can freeze a lump of peanut butter and add it to the middle of the cookie dough before chilling, and then bake for a soft-centred cookie.

NEAPOLITAN COOKIES

Neapolitan ice cream is a classic that everyone has probably enjoyed at some point in their lives. Chocolate, vanilla and strawberry ice cream, all in the same tub, creating the best scoop you can ask for. These flavours, transferred into a cookie dough, just win. It's an incredibly easy dough to make, and then you simply add flavour with vanilla extract, freeze-dried strawberries with a little colouring and cocoa powder.

MAKES: 12

PREP: 45 minutes
CHILL: 30 minutes
BAKE: 11–12 minutes
COOL: 30+ minutes
LASTS: 5+ days,
at room temperature

125g unsalted butter, at room temperature
100g soft light brown sugar
75g white granulated sugar
1 egg
1 tsp vanilla extract
300g plain flour
1½ tsp baking powder
½ tsp bicarbonate of soda
½ tsp sea salt
10g freeze-dried strawberries
½ tsp pink food colouring
25g cocoa powder
2 tbsp whole milk

In a large bowl, beat the butter, light brown sugar and granulated sugar together until creamy. Add the egg and vanilla extract and beat again. Add the plain flour, baking powder, bicarbonate of soda and sea salt and beat until a cookie dough is formed.

In a small food processor, blitz the freeze-dried strawberries to fine crumbs. Portion the cookie dough into three equal lumps of dough, about 225g each. Add one lump of cookie dough back into the original bowl, then add the blitzed strawberries and pink food colouring and beat well until combined. Remove the pink cookie dough from the bowl, then add another lump of plain cookie dough. Add the cocoa powder and milk and beat until combined.

Separate each flavour of cookie dough into 12 pieces. Carefully press together a piece of each flavour, and lightly roll into a cookie dough ball. Chill the cookies in the fridge for 30 minutes. While the cookies are chilling, preheat the oven to 190°C/170°C fan.

Take the cookies out of the fridge and divide between two large, lined baking trays.

Bake in the oven for 11–12 minutes. Leave to cool on the tray for at least 30 minutes, as they will continue to bake while cooling.

NOTES

- Freeze-dried strawberries can be found in some supermarkets, or online. You can use strawberry flavouring if you prefer, but this often needs ordering online as well. Fresh or frozen strawberries cannot be used.

- Try not to overwork the dough when rolling out the flavours and making the cookies as this may stop them from spreading when baking.

APPLE OATMEAL COOKIES

Apple crumble is such a comfort food classic. It's an everyday delicious treat which I adore, so when you combine it with a cookie, it just gets even better. These cookies have an oaty texture, stuffed with delicious chunks of apple and a hint of cinnamon to boot. They're cosy in cookie form, and I am obsessed.

MAKES: 12

PREP: 45 minutes
BAKE: 13–14 minutes
COOL: 30+ minutes
LASTS: 5+ days,
at room temperature

125g unsalted butter, at room
 temperature
175g soft light brown sugar
1 egg
1 tsp vanilla extract
1 tsp ground cinnamon (optional)
150g plain flour
175g rolled oats
1 tsp baking powder
½ tsp bicarbonate of soda
½ tsp sea salt
150g Bramley apples, chopped
 into 1cm cubes

Preheat the oven to 190°C/170°C fan and line 2–3 large baking trays with parchment paper.

In a large bowl, beat the butter and sugar until creamy. Add the egg and vanilla extract and beat again. Add the cinnamon, flour, oats, baking powder, bicarbonate of soda and sea salt and beat until a cookie dough is formed. Fold through the chopped apple pieces with a spatula.

Using a 5cm cookie scoop, portion 12 cookies onto the lined trays, spaced well apart from each other. Bake in the oven for 13–14 minutes. Leave to cool on the tray for at least 30 minutes, as they will continue to bake while cooling.

NOTES

- *The ground cinnamon is optional, but delicious. You can add more or less depending on your personal preference, or you can swap it for ground ginger or nutmeg.*

- *I use large, rolled oats so that you still get a good texture when the cookies are baked.*

- *I recommend using Bramley or cooking apples so you have a good bite to the apple, as eating apples may become too soft when baked.*

COCONUT NYC COOKIES

Delicious homemade coconut New York-style cookies bring a deliciously coconutty flavour to a classic Jane bake – definitely one of my new favourites. I honestly can't comprehend how I haven't shared this recipe sooner – these cookies are so easy, so tasty and if you like coconut, you will adore them. I found using desiccated coconut blended so well with the cookie dough to give the perfect chew, then adding chocolate chips gives you the dreamy coconut-chocolate combo.

MAKES: 8

PREP: 45 minutes
CHILL: 30+ minutes
BAKE: 11–12 minutes
COOL: 30+ minutes
LASTS: 5+ days, at room temperature

125g unsalted butter, at room temperature
100g soft light brown sugar
75g white granulated sugar
1 egg
1 tsp vanilla extract
275g plain flour
75g desiccated coconut
1½ tsp baking powder
½ tsp bicarbonate of soda
½ tsp sea salt
250g milk chocolate chips

In a large bowl, beat the butter, light brown sugar and granulated sugar together until creamy.

Add the egg and vanilla extract and beat again. Add the plain flour, desiccated coconut, baking powder, bicarbonate of soda and sea salt and beat until a cookie dough is formed. Beat in the milk chocolate chips until they are well distributed.

Weigh the cookie dough into eight balls about 125g each. Chill in the freezer for at least 30 minutes, or in the fridge for an hour or so. While the cookies are chilling, preheat the oven to 200°C/180°C fan.

Take the cookies out of the freezer or fridge and divide between two large, lined baking trays.

Bake in the oven for 11–12 minutes. Leave to cool on the tray for at least 30 minutes, as they will continue to bake while cooling.

NOTES

- You can use any flavour of chocolate chips you fancy – I just love the coconut and milk chocolate combination.
- Chopped frozen coconut chocolate bars could also be used instead of chocolate chips.
- You can make the dough chocolate-flavoured by replacing 75g of the plain flour with 50g cocoa powder.

CARAMEL COOKIE CUPS

I love anything cookie or caramel related – I just can't help it. Cookies are my downfall and I have countless cookie recipes like this one on my blog, and in my books, but I still want to show you so many more. These Caramel Cookie Cups bring so many of my favourite things together into a delectable cookie treat, stuffed with caramel and perfect when topped with ice cream, and even an extra little bit of caramel sauce. I'd happily eat these for pudding every day.

MAKES: 12

PREP: 30 minutes
BAKE: 12–14 minutes
COOL: 1 HOUR
LASTS: 3+ days,
at room temperature

115g unsalted butter, melted,
   plus extra for greasing
135g soft light brown sugar
55g granulated sugar
1 egg
1 tsp vanilla extract
275g plain flour, plus extra for
   dusting
1 tsp bicarbonate of soda
½ tsp sea salt
1 tbsp cornflour
200g milk or dark chocolate,
   finely chopped
12 heaped tsp caramel sauce
   (see page 77)

Preheat the oven to 180°C/160°C fan and grease and lightly flour a 12-hole cupcake or muffin tray.

In a large bowl, beat the melted butter, light brown sugar and granulated sugar together for about 2 minutes until creamy. Add the egg and vanilla extract and beat again briefly until smooth. Add the flour, bicarbonate of soda, sea salt and cornflour and beat until a cookie dough is formed. Mix in the finely chopped chocolate with a spatula. Remove 240g cookie dough and set aside. Divide the rest of the dough evenly between the 12 cupcake-tray holes.

Using a spoon, small rolling pin, pastry pusher or similar, push a hole into each ball of cookie dough in the tray. Add the caramel – I use 1 heaped teaspoon per cookie cup.

Split the 240g dough into 20g balls, flatten each one and use to top each cookie cup, pressing down slightly to seal. Bake in the oven for 12–14 minutes. Leave to cool fully in the tray as they're easier to remove once cool.

NOTES

- As caramel doesn't freeze solidly enough to make a stuffed cookie, you must use a cupcake or muffin tray to make these. You can cut small circles of parchment paper to add to the bottom of each hole to help prevent sticking if necessary.

- You can make the cookie dough chocolate-flavoured by replacing 75g of the plain flour with 50g cocoa powder.

HOMEMADE CUSTARD CREAMS

A custard cream is a classic bake that I will always adore. It is one of my favourite biscuits to grab when I am having a cup of tea, and it's a good dunker in my opinion. However, making your own is so easy and so fun. The biscuit dough is really simple, flavoured with custard powder, rolled flat, cut into shapes, chilled and baked. A deliciously easy custard-flavoured buttercream fills each biscuit to create a homemade version of the ever-popular classic.

MAKES: 25

PREP: 1 hour
BAKE: 10–11 minutes
COOL: 1 hour
DECORATE: 30 minutes
LASTS: 3+ days,
at room temperature

200g unsalted butter, at room temperature
100g caster sugar
2 tsp vanilla extract
300g plain flour, plus extra for dusting
125g instant custard powder
2–4 tbsp whole milk

Filling

150g unsalted butter, at room temperature
300g icing sugar
25g instant custard powder
2 tsp vanilla extract
2–4 tbsp whole milk

In a large bowl, beat the butter and sugar together well. Add the vanilla extract, plain flour and instant custard powder and start to beat together, adding the milk slowly so that the dough combines. Roughly shape the dough into a rectangle, wrap with clingfilm and chill for 30 minutes. Towards the end of the 30 minutes, preheat the oven to 180°C/160°C fan and line 2–3 large baking trays with parchment paper.

Place the chilled dough on a lightly floured work surface. Roll the dough into a large rectangle about ½cm thick. Cut the dough into 50 small rectangles with a cutter measuring about 5 x 2.5cm. Carefully place each biscuit onto the lined trays, spaced slightly apart. Bake in the oven for 10–11 minutes until golden. Leave to cool on the trays.

Filling

In a large bowl, beat the butter for several minutes to loosen it. Add the icing sugar and instant custard powder and beat together again. Add the vanilla extract and 1 tablespoon of milk at a time until you reach a smooth and pipeable consistency. Transfer to a piping bag with the piping nozzle of your choice fitted and pipe a small amount of custard buttercream onto half the biscuits. Sandwich each one with another biscuit and enjoy!

NOTES

- You can shape the biscuits however you like – I made rectangles as I wanted a classic shape, but you can make squares, circles, or even use a biscuit cutter to make random shapes like stars.

- You can add more flavour to these biscuits if you want, but I like them as they are. One teaspoon of almond extract is a delicious addition.

CHOCOLATE HAZELNUT CHEESECAKE BROWNIES

So many people think I get bored of baking; but I really don't. Brownies, however, are definitely up there as one of my favourite bakes. Of course, you all know how much I love cheesecake as well, so just like my Chocolate Cheesecake Muffins on page 44, these mash up two bakes to create something utterly glorious. A thick and fudgy brownie mixed with an easy baked vanilla cheesecake and swirls of chocolate hazelnut spread takes these to another level of heaven.

MAKES: 16

PREP: 30 minutes
BAKE: 28–30 minutes
COOL: 1 hour
SET: 3+ hours
LASTS: 3+ days,
in the fridge

200g dark chocolate
200g unsalted butter
4 eggs
275g caster sugar
50g cocoa powder
100g plain flour
200g chocolate hazelnut spread
   (I use Nutella)

Cheesecake

250g full-fat soft cheese
100g caster sugar
1 egg
1 tsp vanilla extract

Preheat the oven to 180°C/160°C fan and line a 23cm square tin with parchment paper.

In a heatproof bowl, break up the dark chocolate into pieces and add the butter. Melt together in the microwave in shorts bursts or over a pan of simmering water (bain-marie), until smooth. Set aside to cool to room temperature.

In a separate bowl, whisk the eggs and sugar together for a few minutes until pale, very mousse-like and doubled in volume. Pour over the cooled chocolate mixture and fold together carefully. Once completely combined, add the cocoa powder and flour and fold together again, still being careful not to knock out the air.

Cheesecake

In a new bowl, beat the soft cheese until loose, then add the sugar and beat again until combined. Gradually beat in the egg until combined, along with the vanilla extract.

Pour 90% of the brownie batter into the tin. Pour the cheesecake mixture on top of the brownie mixture, then dollop on the chocolate hazelnut spread. Add the remaining brownie mixture in dollops and swirl slightly.

Bake in the oven for 28–30 minutes until there is a slight wobble in the middle. Leave to cool completely in the tin, then chill in the fridge for at least 3 hours to set. Cut into squares with a sharp knife.

NOTES

- *The chocolate hazelnut spread can be left out if you just want cheesecake brownies. Or you can mix the spread into the cheesecake mixture to try something a little different.*

CORNFLAKE BROWNIES

A cornflake brownie is one of those bakes that just makes my jaw drop. A wonderfully thick and super-chocolatey brownie mix, topped with an incredibly easy-to-make, cake-like cornflake layer. Honestly, the cornflake layer of these Cornflake Brownies is the sort of thing I make, and before even getting to putting it on the brownies, I just want to devour the entire bowl. The mix of butter, syrup, chocolate and cornflakes is otherworldly, so adding it to a brownie is a simple way to elevate it just by using a storecupboard staple.

MAKES: 16

PREP: 30 minutes
BAKE: 25–30 minutes
COOL: 1 hour
SET: 4+ hours
LASTS: 3+ days,
in the fridge

200g dark chocolate
200g unsalted butter
4 eggs
275g caster sugar
50g cocoa powder
100g plain flour
250g milk chocolate chips

Cornflake Layer

75g unsalted butter
75g golden syrup
300g milk chocolate
150g cornflakes

Preheat the oven to 180°C/160°C fan and line a 23cm square tin with parchment paper.

In a heatproof bowl, break up the dark chocolate into pieces and add the butter. Melt together in the microwave in shorts bursts or over a pan of simmering water (bain-marie), until smooth. Leave to cool to room temperature.

In a separate bowl, whisk the eggs and sugar together for a few minutes until pale, mousse-like and doubled in volume. Pour over the cooled chocolate mixture and fold together carefully. Once completely combined, add the cocoa powder and flour and then fold together again. Fold through the chocolate chips.

Pour the brownie mixture into the tin and bake in the oven for 25–30 minutes until there is an ever so slight wobble in the middle. Leave to cool completely in the tin.

Cornflake Layer

In a medium pan, melt the butter and golden syrup together over a medium heat until combined. Remove the pan from the heat and add the milk chocolate. Stir together, still off the heat, until the mixture is smooth. Pour the cornflakes into a large bowl, pour the chocolate mixture over the top and stir to combine. Pour the cornflake mixture over the brownie and level it. Chill in the fridge for at least 4 hours to set, then cut into squares with a sharp knife.

NOTES

- It's important to let the brownies chill for enough time so that they stay fudgy, and the cornflake layer has enough time to set.
- Even though these are called Cornflake Brownies, you can use other cereals such as rice pops if you want to try something different.

CARROT CAKE BLONDIES

I don't know why the idea of carrot cake blondies isn't a bigger thing yet! Carrot cake is my favourite cake and adding a sweet but delicious blondie into the mix is just spectacular. I love the addition of the carrot cake spices in this recipe as the ginger, cinnamon and nutmeg complement the carrot part of the bake so well. The spices also give such a tasty warmth to the blondies, while the perfect sweetness comes from the white chocolate.

MAKES: 16

PREP: 30 minutes
BAKE: 25–30 minutes
COOL: 1 hour
SET: 2+ hours
LASTS: 3+ days,
at room temperature

175g unsalted butter, melted
250g soft light brown sugar
3 eggs
1 tsp vanilla extract
½ tsp ground ginger
½ tsp ground cinnamon
½ tsp ground nutmeg
1 tsp mixed spice
275g plain flour
175g grated carrot
200g white chocolate chips
 (optional)

Preheat the oven to 180°C/160°C fan and line a 23cm square tin with parchment paper.

In a large bowl, beat the melted butter and sugar together until smooth. Add the eggs and vanilla extract and beat again until smooth. Add the ground ginger, ground cinnamon, ground nutmeg, mixed spice and flour and beat together until you have a thick blondie mixture. Add the grated carrots and chocolate chips, if using, and stir through. Pour the mixture into the tin and spread.

Bake in the oven for 25–30 minutes, or until there is an ever so slight wobble in the middle. Leave the blondies to cool in the tin, then chill in the fridge for at least 2 hours, but preferably overnight. Cut into squares with a sharp knife.

NOTES

- *Leave the blondies to set for as long as you can in the fridge to create the best texture – overnight is best if you can wait that long.*

- *The white chocolate chips are optional, but delicious!*

NO-BAKE CHOCOLATE OAT SLICES

I know people often say that anything with oats is a healthy treat, but this one? Well, it's jam-packed full of butter, sugar, chocolate and peanut butter… so you decide. I say, it's good for the soul, along with all baking. The butter, sugar and oats mix together so easily, and then adding the layer of melted chocolate and peanut butter in the middle of all the oats creates a beautiful tray of chocolate oaty nutty heaven. There's no baking, so the only hard part is waiting for it to set properly, but I promise you – it's worth the wait.

MAKES: 16

PREP: 45 minutes
SET: 2+ hours
LASTS: 3+ days,
at room temperature

300g unsalted butter
140g soft light brown sugar
350g rolled oats
200g milk chocolate
125g crunchy or smooth peanut
    butter

Line a 23cm square tin with parchment paper.

In a medium pan, melt the butter and sugar together over a low-medium heat until smooth. Pour the rolled oats into a large bowl, then pour over the butter mixture. Stir together to combine.

In a separate heatproof bowl, add the milk chocolate and peanut butter and microwave in short bursts or set the bowl over a pan of simmering water (bain-marie) until smooth. Pour half of the oat mixture into the bottom of the lined tin. Pour over the chocolate and peanut butter mixture, and then spread. Top with the remaining oat mixture. Chill in the fridge for at least 2 hours, or until set. Cut into squares with a sharp knife and enjoy.

NOTES

- *Other sugars can work in this recipe, but the soft light brown sugar gives it a delicious flavour, so I would recommend sticking to it if you can.*
- *You can swap the peanut butter for other nut butters, or chocolate spreads if you prefer.*

ETON MESS
ROCKY ROAD

This delicious sweet rocky road is endlessly moreish as it brings together so many yummy things. The idea of chocolate, meringue, strawberry and so on may seem a little much, but honestly, they all just complement each other so well. I found using dried strawberry chunks or freeze-dried strawberries gives the best results as you don't want the moisture from fresh or frozen fruit. These can easily be bought online – and any leftovers are fun to add to drinks!

MAKES: 16

PREP: 30 minutes
SET: 2+ hours
LASTS: 3+ days,
at room temperature

500g white chocolate
50g unsalted butter
100g digestive biscuits, chopped
75g mini marshmallows
60g meringue nests, broken
35g dried strawberry chunks

Line a 23cm square tin with parchment paper.

In a heatproof bowl, break up the white chocolate into pieces and add the butter. Melt together in the microwave in shorts bursts or over a pan of simmering water (bain-marie), until smooth.

In a separate large bowl, add the digestive biscuits, marshmallows, meringue nests and dried strawberries. Stir briefly to combine. Pour in the melted chocolate mixture and stir everything together really well. Pour into the lined tin and spread until even. Chill in the fridge for at least 2 hours, or until set. Cut into squares with a sharp knife.

NOTES

- You can use any biscuits you want; I just prefer digestive biscuits.

- Other chocolates will also work, such as milk or dark chocolate, but the white chocolate fits the theme of Eton mess better.

- You can make homemade meringues (see my recipe for Mini Meringues on page 238), but I find shop-bought meringues perfect as they're often crunchy.

BAKEWELL FLAPJACKS

Bakewell is by far the best combination of flavours in my opinion, and I use it to add a classic twist to as many bakes as I possibly can. The Bakewell Blondies on my blog are one of my favourite bakes ever, but this flapjack version is just as good. Flapjacks are a staple everyday bake, so adding flaked almonds, almond extract and dollops of raspberry jam is a simple way to jazz them up. I decorated my flapjacks as I just couldn't resist, and it was a reason to add even more almonds, so why not give it a go?

MAKES: 12

PREP: 30 minutes
BAKE: 22–25 minutes
COOL: 1 hour
DECORATE: 30 minutes
LASTS: 3+ days,
at room temperature

200g unsalted butter
200g soft light brown sugar
200g honey or golden syrup
1 tsp almond extract
350g rolled oats
100g flaked almonds
250g raspberry jam

Topping
75g white chocolate, melted
15g flaked almonds

Preheat the oven to 180°C/160°C fan and line a 23cm square tin with parchment paper.

In a medium pan, melt the butter, sugar, honey and almond extract over a low heat until smooth.

In a large bowl, add the rolled oats and flaked almonds, then pour over the melted mixture and stir to combine. Firmly press half of the mixture into the bottom of the tin. Spread on the raspberry jam. Top with the remaining oat mixture and level. Bake in the oven for 22–25 minutes until it is starting to brown around the edges and firming up. Leave to cool fully in the tin.

Topping
Carefully drizzle the melted white chocolate over the flapjacks. Toast the almonds in a dry frying pan over a medium heat, stirring often, for a few minutes until golden. Sprinkle over the flapjacks and leave to set in the fridge. Cut into squares with a sharp knife and enjoy.

NOTES
- The raspberry jam can be swapped for other flavours, such as strawberry or cherry, or any you fancy – or you can use 150g fresh raspberries instead.

SALTED CARAMEL NUT SLICES

We all love the combination of salt and sweet right?! Well, to be fair, I know a few people who don't, but as soon as you add in something nutty it brings everyone together. This is a blog favourite inspired by the classic Millionaire's Shortbread but brought up to a whole new level with any nuts you fancy on top of the caramel, plus a little sprinkling of sea salt, and then a drizzle of chocolate on top. Delightful.

MAKES: 16

PREP: 1 hour
BAKE: 20–25 minutes
COOL: 2 hours
DECORATE: 10 minutes
SET: 2 hours
LASTS: 5+ days,
at room temperature

200g unsalted butter
100g caster sugar
300g plain flour

Salted Caramel

200g unsalted butter
3 tbsp caster sugar
4 tbsp golden syrup
397g tin condensed milk
1–2 tsp sea salt flakes

Topping

200g nuts (I use macadamia, hazelnuts, pecans), chopped
75g dark chocolate, melted

Preheat the oven to 180°C/160°C fan, and line a deep 23cm square tin with parchment paper.

In a large bowl, cream the butter and sugar together until smooth. Add the flour and beat until a dough is formed. Firmly press the mixture into the bottom of the tin and bake in the oven for 20–25 minutes until pale golden on top. Leave to cool fully.

Salted Caramel

In a large pan, melt the butter, sugar, golden syrup and condensed milk over a low-medium heat until the sugar has dissolved, stirring constantly to stop anything from catching. Once the sugar has dissolved, turn up the heat to high and let the mixture come to the boil. Boil for 5–7 minutes, stirring constantly so that the mixture doesn't catch. Once the caramel has thickened and turned a deeper golden colour, stir in the sea salt carefully, and pour the caramel onto the shortbread base.

Topping

Sprinkle over the chopped nuts, and drizzle over the melted chocolate. Leave to set in the fridge for a couple of hours, then cut into squares with a sharp knife and enjoy.

NOTES

- I use a combination of my favourite nuts, and whatever I have in the cupboard. If you like one particular nut, then go for it – or just use a combination like me.

- The salt is completely optional if you don't like salted caramel or salty bakes.

- I recommend using butter (rather than margarine or baking spread) for the shortbread and caramel for best results.

LEMON BARS

These five-ingredient bars of fruity heaven are a classic everyday bake, and a fan favourite. The shortbread base is so easy to put together, and then topped with an insanely easy baked lemon curd topping, what could be better? Honestly, these bars will change your life.

MAKES: 16

PREP: 30 minutes
BAKE: 40–50 minutes
COOL: 4+ hours
LASTS: 3+ days,
at room temperature

200g unsalted butter
100g caster sugar
300g plain flour

Topping

375g caster sugar
50g plain flour
6 eggs
225ml lemon juice
Zest of 5 lemons
1–2 tbsp icing sugar

Preheat the oven to 180°C/160°C fan and line a deep 23cm square tin with parchment paper.

In a large bowl, cream the butter and sugar together until smooth. Add the flour and beat until a dough is formed. Firmly press the mixture into the bottom of the tin and bake in the oven for 20–25 minutes until pale golden on top.

Topping

In a bowl, combine the sugar and flour with a whisk. Add the eggs, lemon juice and lemon zest and whisk again until combined.

Once the shortbread is baked, remove from the oven and pour the lemon mixture over the top. Return to the oven and bake for 20–25 minutes until the lemon mixture no longer wobbles. Leave the lemon bars to cool at room temperature for about 2 hours, then chill in the fridge for another 2 hours (or preferably overnight). Serve with a dusting of icing sugar.

NOTES

- Change these up by using other citrus fruits such as orange, or even lime.
- If you don't want to use real lemons, you can use bottled lemon juice and leave out the lemon zest.

Tarts, Pies and Pastries

MEDITERRANEAN VEGETABLE TART

I adore anything which involves roasted vegetables, but especially when it has hints of the Mediterranean. This delightful tart uses all of my favourite vegetables roasted together with some herbs, placed onto a puff pastry base with sun-dried tomato paste and cherry tomatoes – delicious. I love having this for dinner on a busy day with a side salad, or even as a quick everyday lunch.

SERVES: 6

PREP: 15 minutes
ROAST: 15–20 minutes
BAKE: 20–25 minutes
COOL: 10 minutes
LASTS: 2 days, in the fridge (but best served fresh)

2 peppers, cut into 2cm chunks
1 red onion, cut into 2cm chunks
1 courgette, cut into 2cm chunks
3 garlic cloves, crushed
Pinch of salt and pepper
1 tbsp dried rosemary
1 tbsp dried thyme
2 tbsp olive oil
1 x 350g sheet of puff pastry
2 tbsp sun-dried tomato paste
200g cherry tomatoes, halved
1 tbsp milk

Preheat the oven to 220°C/200°C fan and get a large roasting tray ready.

Add the chopped peppers, red onion and courgette to the tray, along with the crushed garlic, salt, pepper, rosemary and thyme. Drizzle over the olive oil and toss together. Roast in the oven for 15–20 minutes until the vegetables are starting to soften.

Unroll the puff pastry sheet onto a large, lined baking tray, and score a 2cm border (don't cut all the way through). Spread the sun-dried tomato paste onto the pastry and top with the roasted vegetables, then add the cherry tomatoes. Brush the milk over the pastry border. Bake in the oven for 20–25 minutes until the pastry is golden.

NOTES

- For an extra little pizazz, sprinkle over 100–200g feta chunks.
- You can swap the vegetables for any you prefer, just keep a similar quantity.
- The herbs are also my personal favourites, so you can switch them up if you want – adding in some chilli flakes gives a delicious spice to the tart.

MUSHROOM, LEEK AND POTATO PIE

When you want a meal that is comforting, warm but also light, this pie is your answer. A delicious veggie filling, topped with crispy filo pastry gives the perfect balance. You can use other veggies, of course, or even leftover veggies from your dinner the night before, so it's great for using up whatever you have in the fridge, but my favourites are mushrooms, leeks and potatoes. A simple cream sauce flavoured with mustard mixed with vegetable stock transforms the dish into something spectacular.

SERVES: 6–8
PREP: 30 minutes
BAKE: 25 minutes
LASTS: Best served fresh

400g baby chestnut mushrooms
2 leeks, finely sliced
Knob of butter
300g cooked new potatoes, chopped into quarters
3 garlic cloves, crushed
Pinch of salt and pepper
250ml vegetable stock
1 tsp wholegrain mustard
150ml double cream
7 sheets of filo pastry
Olive oil
½ tbsp sesame seeds

Preheat the oven to 200°C/180°C fan and grab a round baking dish.

Add the mushrooms and leeks to a large frying pan with the butter and fry until they are starting to soften. Add the potatoes, along with the garlic, salt and pepper. Pour in the vegetable stock, mustard and double cream and mix to combine. Boil for a few minutes until the mixture starts to thicken. Pour into your dish.

Crumple separate sheets of filo pastry in your hands and place on top of the mixture to cover. Spray the pastry with a little oil and sprinkle it with sesame seeds. Bake in the oven for about 25 minutes, or until golden brown. Serve hot with salad for a delicious meal.

NOTES

- *You can add 100g spinach to the mixture to increase the greens.*
- *You can also add 1 teaspoon of mixed herbs to switch up the sauce.*

CHICKEN, LEEK AND BACON PIE

When I want something cosy and comforting to curl up with on a cold day, I always think of a recipe like this fan favourite. I flavour my sauce with thyme and bay leaves, but you can do what you prefer. Of course, the winner in this dish is the puff pastry because as soon as that's involved, I am obsessed. I love to serve this with a salad and new potatoes for lunch, or roasted potatoes and green veg for dinner.

SERVES: 6–8

PREP: 30 minutes
BAKE: 40 minutes
LASTS: Best
served fresh

2 x sheets of puff pastry
200g bacon lardons
2 medium leeks, sliced
600g chicken breast, cut into
   chunks
1 tsp dried thyme
5 bay leaves
200ml chicken stock
150ml double cream
1 tbsp cornflour, dissolved
   in 2 tbsp cold water
Salt and pepper
Milk, to glaze

Preheat the oven to 200°C/180°C fan and grab a 35 x 23cm pie dish.

Line the base and sides of the dish with one of the sheets of puff pastry. Line the pastry with some parchment paper and fill with baking beans. Bake in the oven for 15 minutes to prevent a soggy bottom. The pastry might puff up slightly along the sides but that's fine. Remove the parchment and baking beans.

While you are baking the pastry, fry the bacon lardons in a large frying pan over a medium heat until they have started to turn crispy – this is to cook the fat off. Pour the lardons into a bowl. Add the leeks to the frying pan and fry until they have started to soften slightly. Add the chicken chunks and fry for a few minutes. Return the cooked bacon lardons to the pan, along with the dried thyme, bay leaves, chicken stock, double cream and cornflour mixture. Bring to a rolling boil, stirring so that the mixture thickens. Season with salt and pepper. Pour the mixture into the pie dish on top of the baked pastry.

Top the pie with your second sheet of puff pastry – I sealed the pastry around the sides of the dish by pressing it in with my thumbs. Cut a small cross into the middle of the pie so that the air has somewhere to escape. Brush the pastry with a little milk to glaze it slightly and decorate with extra pieces of puff pastry from the offcuts if you fancy. Bake in the oven for about 25 minutes, or until it is golden brown. Serve hot with salad, or potatoes and green veg.

NOTES

- *You can swap the chicken stock for vegetable stock if you prefer – and switch the chicken and bacon for mushrooms and extra leeks if you want a vegetarian pie.*

MINI QUICHES

I love quiche, especially my Bacon, Brie and Tomato Quiche on page 91, but anything bite-sized has my heart. I finally decided on creating a mini quiche recipe after endless requests, including some different filling suggestions. Each flavour idea works for all 12 Mini Quiches, but you can use smaller amounts to make a variety of flavours if you prefer, or even mash them up to make a new flavour. These are delicious served as part of a picnic, lunch or dinner and they can be prepped in advance and enjoyed hot or cold.

MAKES: 12

PREP: 1 hour
BAKE: 18–22 minutes
COOL: 1 hour
LASTS: 3+ days,
in the fridge

Butter, for greasing
Plain flour, for dusting
1 x 350g sheet of shortcrust pastry
175ml double cream
2 eggs
Salt and pepper

Quiche Lorraine

15g unsalted butter
100g finely chopped bacon, fat
    removed
½ onion, finely chopped
50g mature Cheddar cheese,
    finely grated

Spinach and pepper

100g spinach
1 red pepper, finely chopped
50g mature Cheddar cheese,
    finely grated

Preheat the oven to 200°C/180°C fan. Grease and flour a 12-hole muffin tray.

On a floured work surface, unroll the sheet of shortcrust pastry and cut out 8–9cm circles with a cutter. Press into the muffin holes. Whisk together the double cream, eggs, salt and pepper.

Quiche Lorraine

Heat a frying pan over a medium heat, then add the butter, bacon and onion. Cook until the bacon has started to become crispy. Add spoonfuls of the mixture to the pastry cases, sprinkle over the cheese and pour over the egg mixture.

Spinach and pepper

Add the spinach to a frying pan over a low heat and cook until wilted. Add the spinach and red pepper to the pastry cases, sprinkle over the cheese and pour over the egg mixture.

Mushroom

Heat a frying pan over a medium heat, then add the butter and the mushrooms and cook until they have started to soften. Divide between the pastry cases, sprinkle over the cheese and pour over the egg mixture.

Bake in the oven for 18–22 minutes until the cheese has turned golden and the quiches are starting to brown. Leave to cool in the tin, then enjoy.

Mushroom

15g unsalted butter

100g baby chestnut mushrooms, chopped small

50g mature Cheddar cheese, finely grated

NOTES ⁓

- You can make your own shortcrust pastry using my recipe on page 91.

- Feel free to use other filling ideas, just try and stick to the same quantities as they really are mini.

- You might find it best to line the base of the muffin tray with small circles of parchment paper to help prevent sticking if you are worried.

BACON, BRIE AND TOMATO QUICHE

There's something special about a bit of savoury baking, and a quiche is one of the best things to choose. The pastry is so much easier to make than people think, and you can prepare it ahead of time and chill in the fridge until needed, so it's ready to whip up a tasty lunch. This blog favourite includes crispy bacon lardons, tomatoes and lots of cheese – I hope you love it as much as I do.

SERVES: 8–10+

PREP: 90 minutes
BAKE: 40–45 minutes
CHILL: 1 hour
LASTS: 3+ days,
in the fridge

175g plain flour, plus extra for dusting
75g chilled unsalted butter, cubed, plus extra for greasing
Pinch of sea salt
1–3 tbsp cold water

Filling

300g bacon lardons
200g brie
250ml double cream
3 eggs
Salt and pepper
300g cherry tomatoes
75g mature Cheddar cheese, grated

Grease and flour a 23cm tart tin.

Add the flour, butter and sea salt to a bowl and rub together with your fingertips until it resembles breadcrumbs. Add the water 1 tablespoon at a time, mixing and kneading well with your hands until the dough comes together, using as little water as possible.

On a lightly floured work surface, roll out the pastry until 3mm thick. Carefully press the pastry into the tin, making sure to press into the sides very well. I do not cut off the overhang of pastry. Chill the pastry case in the fridge while the oven preheats to 200°C/180°C fan.

Line the pastry case with parchment paper and fill with baking beans, or uncooked rice.

Bake in the oven for 15 minutes, then remove the parchment paper and beans or rice and bake for a further 5 minutes. Leave to cool for 10 minutes, then trim off the excess pastry with a sharp knife to create the perfect pastry case.

Filling

In a frying pan, cook the bacon lardons until they are cooked through and crispy. Spread these on the bottom of the pastry case. Slice the brie into 3mm-thick slices, and layer across the bottom of the pastry case.

In a small bowl, whisk together the double cream, eggs and some salt and pepper. Pour this over the brie. Top the quiche with the cherry tomatoes, and sprinkle over the cheese.

Bake in the oven for 20–25 minutes until golden and only wobbling slightly in the middle. Leave to cool for 20 minutes before removing from the tin. Enjoy warm or leave to cool completely and serve cold.

HOMEMADE PASTIES

We've all seen and appreciated a pasty, right?! I can't help myself. They are one of those things that if I smell them freshly baked, I want to buy the lot and just sit and enjoy myself... But something about homemade pasties makes them even better. I've gone as classic as I can with helpful notes from my granny's old recipes. I love to make these in advance and reheat them for my lunches, or even enjoy as a picnic. You can also freeze them, so they're there whenever you need one. Of course, that's if you can stop yourself from eating them fresh out of the oven.

MAKES: 4 large

PREP: 45 minutes
BAKE: 45 minutes
COOL: 10 minutes
LASTS: 3+ days,
at room temperature

500g plain flour, plus extra for
   dusting
115g lard
115g unsalted butter, cold and
   cubed
1 egg, plus 1 beaten, to glaze
4–6 tbsp water

Filling

300g beef skirt, in small cubes
400g potato, peeled and diced
175g swede, peeled and diced
1 large onion, finely chopped
Pinch of salt and pepper

In a food processor, blitz the flour, lard, butter and egg together. Gradually add the water while blitzing until it starts to combine. Alternatively, rub the flour, lard, butter and egg together with your fingertips and gradually add the water and combine with your hands. Knead the dough into a ball and then divide into four. Wrap in clingfilm and chill for 15 minutes.

Filling

Preheat the oven to 220°C/200°C fan and line two large baking trays with parchment paper.

While the pastry is chilling, add the beef, potato, swede, onion, salt and pepper to a bowl and mix to combine.

On a lightly floured surface, roll each pastry ball into a large circle about 20–23cm in size. Dollop a quarter of the filling mixture onto each pastry circle. Dip your finger into water and wet the edges of the pastry slightly. Bring the pastry together and seal by crimping the edges together.

Place two pasties onto each tray and brush with the egg to glaze. Bake in the oven for 10 minutes, then reduce the temperature to 180°C/160°C fan and bake for a further 35 minutes. Leave to cool for 10 minutes before enjoying hot, or cool completely.

NOTES

- The pasties can be reheated in the oven at 200°C/180°C fan for 20–25 minutes to enjoy warm again if you have made them ahead of time.

SAUSAGE PLAIT

We all know and love sausage rolls, and the recipe on my blog and in my first book is so popular. However, I was asked over and over for a more showstopping version that you could bake for dinner, or enjoy for a celebration, and here it is. If I could argue the fact that this serves one, I would. It is glorious. Serve it as part of a roast, or even with salad – it's so versatile.

SERVES: 8–10

PREP: 30 minutes
BAKE: 40–45 minutes
COOL: 20 minutes
LASTS: 3+ days
in the fridge

400g sausagemeat
1 red onion, finely chopped
3 garlic cloves, finely chopped
1 small apple, grated (optional)
125g dried breadcrumbs
1 tsp chilli flakes
1 tbsp dried thyme
½ tbsp dried rosemary
Pinch of salt and pepper
Plain flour, for dusting
1 x 350g sheet of puff pastry
1 egg, beaten

Preheat the oven to 210°C/190°C fan and line a large baking tray with parchment paper.

In a bowl, mix the sausagemeat, red onion, garlic, grated apple, breadcrumbs, chilli flakes, thyme, rosemary, salt and pepper with a spatula until combined.

On a lightly floured work surface or the baking tray, unroll the puff pastry sheet. Cut diagonal lines into the pastry on each side (lengthways), leaving a third of the pastry uncut in the middle. Spread the sausage mixture in the middle (where you haven't cut the pastry).

Fold each diagonal strip of pastry over each other, covering the sausage filling with pastry. Seal where the bits of pastry meet with some beaten egg. Brush the top of the sausage plait with more beaten egg.

Bake in the oven for 40–45 minutes until the pastry has puffed up nicely, and the sausagemeat has cooked through. Leave to cool for 20 minutes, then enjoy hot, or cool completely and enjoy cold from the fridge.

NOTES

- The herbs and spices suit my tastes, so feel free to increase or decrease the quantities as you prefer – or even add in something else!
- The apple is optional, but it brings a delicious sweetness to the sausage plait.
- To take it to the next level, add a layer of red onion chutney to the pastry before filling with the sausage mixture.

EASY FRUIT TART

When I want to make something sweet, light and fruity I always think of this beautiful tart. This blog favourite is the perfect pudding for any time of year as you can adapt and change the recipe to suit whatever fruit is in season – just use 500g of any fruit you fancy. I used a no-bake biscuit base for ease, but this tart works really well with pastry – use my recipe for pastry on page 106 (Pumpkin Pie). For the filling, I wanted something sweet and cream-like, so a whipped mascarpone was perfect. The fruit makes a simple but impressive decoration to elevate the everyday.

SERVES: 8–10+

PREP: 30 minutes
SET: 2 hours
LASTS: 3+ days,
in the fridge

300g digestive biscuits
150g unsalted butter, melted

Filling

200ml double cream
250g mascarpone
100g icing sugar
1 tsp vanilla extract

Fruit

100g strawberries
100g kiwi fruit
100g blueberries
100g raspberries
100g blackberries

Blitz the biscuits to a fine crumb in a food processor or crush in a bowl with a rolling pin.

Add the melted butter and mix together. Press into the sides and base of a springform 23cm tart tin.

Filling

In a clean bowl, whisk the double cream, mascarpone, icing sugar and vanilla extract until smooth and starting to thicken. Pour this onto the biscuit base and chill in the fridge while you prep the fruit.

Fruit

Prep the fruit by washing and removing any greenery or skin that you need to. Cut larger fruit, such as strawberries and kiwis, into thin slices. Create rings of each fruit in circles on the tart to make a pretty pattern. Chill for about 2 hours until set, then enjoy!

NOTES

- You can make the base chocolate-flavoured by adding 25g of cocoa powder to the blended biscuits and melted butter.

- You can make the filling chocolate-flavoured by folding through 150g melted chocolate of your choice.

SPECULOOS TART

Can we all appreciate the wonderful caramelised spiced biscuit taste of this blog favourite for a minute? Add this insanely wonderful flavour to a no-bake tart, and you have a simple, easy-to-prep winner. With a speculoos biscuit base, a layer of speculoos spread and then a speculoos-flavoured ganache, this is definitely one for all the speculoos lovers out there.

SERVES: 8–10+

PREP: 30 minutes
SET: 4–5 hours
LASTS: 3+ days,
in the fridge

300g speculoos biscuits (I use Biscoff)
100g unsalted butter, melted

Filling

150g speculoos spread (I use Biscoff)
250ml double cream
125g dark chocolate
125g milk chocolate
50g unsalted butter

Decoration

Speculoos biscuits and crumbs
50g speculoos spread, melted

Blitz the biscuits to a fine crumb in a food processor or crush in a bowl with a rolling pin.

Add the melted butter and mix together. Press into the sides and base of a springform 23cm tart tin.

Filling

Melt the speculoos spread in a heatproof bowl in the microwave until smooth and pour into the biscuit crust.

In a pan, add the double cream and heat until just before boiling point.

In a separate bowl, add the dark chocolate, milk chocolate and butter, then pour over the hot cream. Whisk together until smooth. If the chocolate is not all melted, heat for 10-second bursts in the microwave until combined well. Pour the chocolate mixture onto the biscuit base and chill for 1 hour.

Decoration

Remove from the fridge and decorate with biscuits and biscuit crumbs, drizzle over the melted spread and chill for another 3–4 hours to set. Remove from the tin.

NOTES

- This tart also works with other spreads such as chocolate hazelnut spread or chocolate spread.
- You can make the ganache with just dark chocolate by using 200g total.
- You can make the ganache with just milk chocolate by using 350g total.

TREACLE TART

Just like my Pineapple Upside Down Cake on page 23, this Treacle Tart is another cult classic. Honestly, the number of requests I get from my followers to post a treacle tart is insane! I totally understand because it's the sort of bake you could eat on a daily basis, whether it's served with custard, ice cream or a drizzle of cream. If you've not made a treacle tart before, just trust the process of using breadcrumbs, lemon, syrup, cream and egg in a mixture – it really works!

SERVES: 8–10+

PREP: 30 minutes
BAKE: 45–50 minutes
COOL: 30 minutes
LASTS: 3+ days,
in the fridge

175g plain flour, plus extra for dusting
100g chilled unsalted butter, cubed, plus extra for greasing
1 tbsp icing sugar
1 egg yolk

Filling

500g golden syrup
Zest and juice of 1 lemon
125g white breadcrumbs, made from stale bread
75ml double cream
1 egg

NOTES

- *If you want to create a deeper flavour to your tart, try swapping some of the golden syrup for black treacle. I've tried it with 400g syrup and 100g treacle, and also 300g syrup and 200g treacle and both are delicious.*

Grease and flour a 23cm tart tin.

Add the flour, butter and icing sugar to a bowl and rub together with your fingertips until the mixture resembles breadcrumbs. Add the egg yolk and mix and knead well with your hands until the dough comes together.

On a lightly floured work surface, roll out the pastry until 3mm thick. Carefully press the pastry into the tin, making sure to press into the sides very well, leaving a small overhang of pastry. Save any spare pastry for later. Chill the pastry case in the fridge while the oven preheats to 200°C/180°C fan.

Line the pastry case with parchment paper and fill with baking beans, or uncooked rice.

Bake in the oven for 15 minutes, then remove the parchment paper and beans or rice and bake for a further 5 minutes. Leave to cool for 10 minutes, then trim off the excess pastry with a sharp knife to create the perfect pastry case.

Filling

Pour the golden syrup into a pan, then add the lemon zest and juice. Heat until the golden syrup is hot and thinned, then stir in the breadcrumbs. Leave to cool for 5 minutes.

In a separate bowl, beat the double cream and egg together, then pour in the breadcrumb mixture and beat together. Pour into the baked pastry case, then bake in the oven for 25–30 minutes until golden. Remove from the oven and leave in the tin to cool completely.

BLACK FOREST TART

When I think of black forest flavours, I think of a lot of chocolate and cherry mixed together, maybe with a dash of whipped cream. This Black Forest Tart reimagines that classic combination with a homemade chocolate pastry, where the usual icing sugar is swapped out for cocoa powder, topped with a glorious cherry conserve layer, ganache, then swirls of sweetened cream and even more cherries – taking black forest to a whole new level.

SERVES: 8–10+

PREP: 30 minutes
BAKE: 20 minutes
SET: 1 hour
LASTS: 3+ days
in the fridge

175g plain flour, plus extra for dusting
100g chilled unsalted butter, cubed, plus extra for greasing
1 tbsp cocoa powder
1 egg yolk

Filling

325g cherry jam or conserve
125g dark chocolate
125g milk chocolate
50g unsalted butter
300ml double cream

Topping

300ml double cream
1 tbsp icing sugar
200g cherries
Chocolate shavings

Grease and flour a 23cm tart tin.

Add the flour, butter and cocoa powder to a bowl and rub together with your fingertips until the mixture resembles breadcrumbs. Add the egg yolk and mix and knead well with your hands until the dough comes together. Add a small amount of cold water if you need to bring the dough together further.

On a lightly floured work surface, roll out the pastry until 3mm thick. Carefully press the pastry into the tin, making sure to press into the sides very well, leaving a small overhang of pastry. Save any spare pastry for later. Chill the pastry case in the fridge while the oven preheats to 200°C/180°C fan.

Line the pastry case with parchment paper and fill with baking beans, or uncooked rice.

Bake in the oven for 15 minutes, then remove the parchment paper and beans or rice and bake for a further 5 minutes. Leave to cool for 10 minutes, then trim off the excess pastry with a sharp knife to create the perfect pastry case.

Filling

Spread the cherry jam onto the pastry base. Add the dark chocolate, milk chocolate and unsalted butter to a bowl.

In a small pan, heat the double cream until just before boiling point, then pour it over the chocolate and butter. Stir until melted and smooth. Pour the chocolate mixture over the cherry jam base and set in the fridge for 1 hour.

Topping

Whip the double cream and icing sugar together until soft peaks form. Dollop onto the tart and decorate with the cherries. Sprinkle over some chocolate shavings.

PUMPKIN PIE

I know a pumpkin pie is a classic bake for Halloween because of the pumpkin filling, but I really would eat this all year round. This recipe uses an easy homemade sweet pastry, with one of the easiest pie fillings you will find. Luckily a lot of the ingredients are soft, so you simply mix the filling together in a bowl with a spoon and then pour onto the baked pastry case. I love using leftover pastry as decoration as it really vamps up a pie recipe, and this just looks so pretty!

MAKES: 8–10+

PREP: 45 minutes
BAKE: 60–70 minutes
SET: 1 hour
LASTS: 3+ days,
in the fridge

175g plain flour, plus extra for
  dusting
100g chilled unsalted butter,
  cubed, plus extra for greasing
1 tbsp icing sugar
1 egg yolk

Filling

425g pumpkin purée
100g maple syrup
50g caster sugar
1 tsp mixed spice
½ tsp ground cinnamon
3 eggs
150ml evaporated milk

Grease and flour a 23cm tart tin.

Add the flour, butter and icing sugar to a bowl and rub together with your fingertips until the mixture resembles breadcrumbs. Add the egg yolk and mix and knead well with your hands until the dough comes together.

On a lightly floured work surface, roll out the pastry until 3mm thick. Carefully press the pastry into the tin, making sure to press into the sides very well, leaving a small overhang of pastry. Save any spare pastry for later. Chill in the fridge while the oven preheats to 200°C/180°C fan.

Line the pastry case with parchment paper and fill with baking beans, or uncooked rice. Bake in the oven for 15 minutes, then remove the parchment paper and beans or rice and bake for a further 5 minutes. Leave to cool for 10 minutes, then trim off the excess pastry with a sharp knife to create the perfect pastry case.

Filling

In a large bowl, whisk the pumpkin purée, maple syrup, sugar, mixed spice, cinnamon, eggs and evaporated milk together until smooth. Pour this over the baked pastry base. If you want to decorate the pumpkin pie, carefully cut out shapes from the spare pastry using some pastry cutters and decorate the edge of the shell – I layered leaves of pastry around the edge of my pie. Bake in the oven for 40–50 minutes until the centre of the pumpkin pie stops wobbling. Leave to cool for 20 minutes before removing from the tin.

NOTES

• I use tinned pumpkin purée, which can be found in some shops or online, but you can make your own by roasting 425g pumpkin pieces at 200°C/180°C fan for 40–45 minutes until softened, then blending for 5 minutes until smooth.

BLUEBERRY PIE

Fruity baked pies are always such a warming idea, perfect for colder months, but they can easily be adapted to suit every day of the year by switching up the fruit to whatever is available. This Blueberry Pie has sweetness, sharpness and can be served with cream, ice cream or even custard depending on what you fancy. The decoration of the pastry is part of the fun here. I used strips to create a traditional lattice top, but use cookie cutters or even fondant cutters to create a beautiful pattern if you prefer.

SERVES: 8–10+

PREP: 30 minutes
BAKE: 35–45 minutes
LASTS: 3+ days,
in the fridge

350g plain flour, plus extra for dusting

200g chilled unsalted butter, cubed

2 tbsp icing sugar

1 egg, plus 1 egg, beaten, for glazing

25g soft light brown sugar

Filling

600g blueberries

Zest and juice of 1 lemon

75g caster sugar

25g cornflour

Add the flour, butter and icing sugar to a bowl and rub together with your fingertips until the mixture resembles breadcrumbs. Add the egg and mix in, then knead well until the dough comes together. Wrap in clingfilm and chill for 20 minutes.

Roll out the dough on a lightly floured work surface into a large circle and cut a circle 2.5–5cm bigger than your pie dish (which should be about 23cm in width). Press the circle of pastry into the base and sides of the pie dish and let the overhang sit. Chill while you preheat the oven to 200°C/180°C fan.

Cut out any shapes you want from the leftover pastry – I cut lines of pastry to make a lattice top.

Filling

In a large bowl, mix the blueberries, lemon zest and juice, sugar and cornflour together briefly. Pour into the chilled pastry case and then decorate with the extra pastry. Trim the pastry to the sides of the pie dish and brush the pastry with the beaten egg. Sprinkle over the brown sugar. Bake in the oven for 35–45 minutes, or until golden. Leave to cool for 10 minutes before serving.

NOTES

• If you're short on time, you can use 500g ready-made shortcrust pastry.

• You can swap the blueberries for other berries such as blackberries, raspberries, strawberries or use a mixture.

APPLE TURNOVERS

An apple turnover is simply puff pastry encasing an easy yet delicious mixture of cooking apples, sugar, cinnamon and butter – with a glaze of milk and a dusting of sugar for a little crunch and looks. You can eat these as they are, especially if you like them warm, or you can serve them with a dollop of ice cream or thick cream for something a little more spectacular. They can also be frozen (see Notes below), so are great for a make-ahead option.

MAKES: 4

PREP: 20 minutes
BAKE: 15–18 minutes
COOL: 15 minutes
LASTS: 2+ days, in the fridge (but best served fresh)

2 medium Bramley apples, peeled, cored and cut into small chunks
50g soft light brown sugar, plus 2 tsp for sprinkling
1 tsp ground cinnamon
15g unsalted butter
1 x 350g sheet of puff pastry
Plain flour, for dusting
Whole milk, for glazing
Icing sugar, for dusting

Add the apples to a small pan, along with the sugar, cinnamon and 1 tablespoon of water. Cover and simmer for 8–10 minutes until the apples have started to break down. Stir through the butter until it has melted. Leave to cool fully.

Preheat the oven to 220°C/200°C fan and line a large baking tray with parchment paper.

Unroll the puff pastry sheet onto a floured work surface and cut it into four rectangles. Dollop the apple mixture onto one half of each of the rectangles, leaving a 1cm border of pastry on show. Brush the pastry borders with milk and fold the pastry over and seal together with your fingers or a fork. Brush the tops of the turnovers with more milk, and sprinkle over some sugar.

Transfer the turnovers to the large baking tray and bake in the oven for 15–18 minutes until golden. Leave to cool for at least 15 minutes to enjoy fresh, or cool fully to enjoy cold. Dust with icing sugar before serving.

NOTES

- You can jazz up the flavours by using half apple and half blackberries. Add the blackberries to the apple mixture just before putting in the pastries – they don't need cooking down.

- You can prepare the apple filling, cool it and place it into the pastries. If you like, you can then freeze the turnovers at this stage and bake as and when you want them. Simply glaze before baking and add 2 minutes to the baking time.

Puddings and Desserts

CARROT CAKE CHEESECAKE

Combining classic bakes is one of my favourite things to do, so why not mix
very-popular carrot cake with a layer of cheesecake? This blog favourite is SO GOOD!
Carrot cake works so well with soft cheese frosting, so why not take it to an entirely
new level with a layer of delicious, spiced cheesecake? Carrot cake keeps
wonderfully in the fridge, so it really is a match made in heaven.

SERVES: 12

PREP: 30 minutes
BAKE: 30–35 minutes
COOL: 2 hours
SET: 5–6+ hours
DECORATE: 20 minutes
LASTS: 3+ days,
in the fridge

125ml sunflower or vegetable oil

3 eggs

150g soft light brown sugar

225g grated carrots

75g raisins (optional)

Zest of 1 orange

175g self-raising flour

¾ tsp bicarbonate of soda

1 tsp mixed spice

½ tsp ground cinnamon

½ tsp ground ginger

Cheesecake

500g full-fat soft cheese

1 tsp orange extract

½ tsp ground cinnamon

½ tsp ground ginger

½ tsp mixed spice

75g icing sugar

300ml double cream

Decoration

150ml double cream

2 tbsp icing sugar

75g chopped walnuts

Preheat the oven to 180°C/160°C fan and line a deep 20cm cake tin
with parchment paper.

Pour the oil into a bowl with the eggs, sugar, grated carrots,
raisins (if using) and orange zest. Mix together with a spatula
until combined. Add the flour, bicarbonate of soda, mixed spice,
cinnamon and ginger and mix again until just combined. Pour into
the tin and bake in the oven for 30–35 minutes. Leave to cool fully
in the tin.

Cheesecake

In a large bowl, whisk the soft cheese, orange extract, cinnamon,
ginger, mixed spice and icing sugar together. Pour in the double
cream and whisk until thickened. Alternatively, whisk the cream in
a separate bowl and then fold through the cheesecake mixture.
Spread the mixture over the top of the cooled carrot cake. Set in the
fridge for at least 5–6 hours.

Decoration

Whip the double cream and icing sugar together until soft peaks
form. Transfer to a piping bag with the piping nozzle of your choice
fitted and pipe onto the cheesecake however you fancy. Decorate
with the chopped walnuts.

NOTES

- You can add chopped nuts to the carrot cake mixture if you want to
  create texture, and the raisins are 100% optional if you don't like them.

- If you prefer other spices or ratios of spices, adapt them to suit your
  preference – ½ teaspoon of nutmeg or allspice or mixed spice work
  very well.

- Full-fat soft cheese is great here, but the sweetness of full-fat
  mascarpone would also complement the other flavours in the
  cheesecake perfectly.

WHITE CHOCOLATE CHEESECAKE

There is something so wonderfully simple about a no-bake treat like this cheesecake. This sweet fan favourite is super easy to put together and prep in advance so you can enjoy it for pudding that evening. I love the simplicity of the white chocolate flavour as it brings a punch and sweetness that you sometimes don't get from a shop-bought cheesecake. One of the greats things about a no-bake treat like this is that you can jazz it up using whatever biscuit you prefer (or have in your cupboard) – ginger nuts are a personal favourite. You can also add in 1 teaspoon of lemon extract for a flavour twist.

SERVES: 12

PREP: 30 minutes
SET: 5–6+ hours
DECORATE: 20 minutes
LASTS: 3+ days,
in the fridge

300g digestive biscuits
100g unsalted butter, melted

Cheesecake

300g white chocolate (I use
    Milkybar)
500g full-fat soft cheese
75g icing sugar
1 tsp vanilla extract
300ml double cream

Decoration

50g white chocolate, melted
150ml double cream
2 tbsp icing sugar
White chocolate pieces

Blitz the biscuits to a fine crumb in a food processor or crush in a bowl with a rolling pin. Add the melted butter and mix together. Press into the base of a 20cm springform cake tin.

Cheesecake

Add the white chocolate to a heatproof bowl and melt until smooth. You can do this in the microwave in short bursts, stirring well each time, or in a bowl over a pan of simmering water. Leave to cool for 5 minutes.

In a new bowl, whisk the soft cheese, icing sugar and vanilla extract together in a stand mixer until combined. Pour in the melted and cooled white chocolate and whisk again on a low speed until combined. Pour in the double cream and whisk until thickened. Alternatively, whisk the double cream in a separate bowl and then fold through the cheesecake mixture. Spread the mixture over the biscuit base. Set in the fridge for at least 5–6 hours or overnight.

Decoration

Remove the cheesecake from the tin and place on a serving plate. Drizzle over the melted white chocolate. Whip the double cream and icing sugar together until soft peaks form. Transfer to a piping bag with the piping nozzle of your choice fitted and pipe onto the cheesecake in big swirls or however you fancy. Add a piece of white chocolate to each cream swirl.

NOTES

- The chocolate must be completely cool before using in the recipe.
- You can add raspberries, strawberries or similar if you want a fruitier (no) bake!

MINI SPECULOOS CHEESECAKES

We all know how much I love cheesecake, right?! I have nearly 100 cheesecake recipes across my website and three books now and I wonder if I have some sort of obsession – but I don't think there is anything wrong with that! I also adore all things speculoos (as you all know as well), so when you stuff speculoos into a mini cheesecake, you cannot go wrong. Mini cheesecakes are easy to make, quicker to set than a regular one and also simple to plop on a plate and devour for an easy, everyday sweet treat.

MAKES: 12

PREP: 30 minutes
SET: 3–4+ hours
DECORATE: 20 minutes
LASTS: 3+ days,
in the fridge

200g speculoos biscuits
   (I use Biscoff)
75g unsalted butter, melted

Filling

300g full-fat soft cheese
50g icing sugar
½ tsp vanilla extract
150g speculoos spread (I use
   Biscoff)
150g double cream

Decoration

35g speculoos spread, melted
125ml double cream
1 tbsp icing sugar
12 speculoos biscuits
Sprinkles

Blitz the biscuits to a fine crumb in a food processor or crush in a bowl with a rolling pin. Add the melted butter and mix together. Press into the bases of a 12-hole mini cake tray.

Filling

In a large bowl, whisk the soft cheese, icing sugar and vanilla extract together until combined. Add the speculoos spread and whisk again. Pour in the double cream and whisk until thickened. Alternatively, whisk the cream in a separate bowl and then fold through the cheesecake mixture. Dollop or pipe the mixture onto the 12 mini cheesecake bases evenly and smooth over. Set in the fridge for at least 3–4 hours.

Decoration

Remove the mini cheesecakes from the tin. Drizzle over the melted speculoos spread.

Whip the double cream and icing sugar together until soft peaks form. Transfer to a piping bag with the piping nozzle of your choice fitted and pipe onto the cheesecakes however you fancy.

Add a speculoos biscuit to each cheesecake and some sprinkles if you like.

NOTES

* Mini cake moulds can vary slightly in size, so this recipe may make a few less or more cheesecakes, depending on your tin.

* You can swap the speculoos biscuits for another type, such as digestive biscuits, if you prefer.

PASSION FRUIT CHEESECAKE

Using passion fruit in my bakes is becoming an increasingly popular idea, and I am UTTERLY IN LOVE with this Passion Fruit Cheesecake. The gingernut biscuits in the base bring a delightful warming flavour, but you can use a regular digestive biscuit base if you prefer or that's what you have in the cupboard. The cheesecake is flavoured with citrus, then topped with the most delicious passion fruit jelly and decoration you will find. Not only is passion fruit one of my favourite flavours, but I also think they look so pretty for decoration on a dessert like this.

SERVES: 12

PREP: 45 minutes
SET: 5–6+ hours
DECORATE: 20 minutes
LASTS: 3+ days,
in the fridge

300g gingernut biscuits
100g unsalted butter, melted
12g powdered gelatine
75ml boiling water
250g passion fruit purée

Filling

400g full-fat soft cheese
100g icing sugar
1 tsp vanilla extract
Zest of ½ lemon
Zest of ½ orange
300ml double cream

Decoration

150ml double cream
2 tbsp icing sugar
3–4 passion fruit segments
and pulp

Blitz the biscuits to a fine crumb in a food processor or crush in a bowl with a rolling pin. Add the melted butter and mix together. Press into the base of a 20cm springform cake tin.

Pour the gelatine into a jug with the boiling water and stir until the gelatine dissolves into a smooth paste. Add the passion fruit purée and stir until smooth. Set aside for now, stirring often so it doesn't begin to set.

Filling

In a large bowl, whisk the soft cheese, icing sugar, vanilla extract, lemon and orange zests together until combined. Pour in the double cream and whisk until thickened. Alternatively, whisk the cream in a separate bowl and then fold through the cheesecake mixture. Spread the mixture over the biscuit base. Carefully pour the passion fruit jelly mixture over the top. Set in the fridge for at least 5–6 hours or overnight.

Decoration

Remove the cheesecake from the tin and place on a serving plate. Whip the double cream and icing sugar together until soft peaks form and dollop onto the jelly layer. Add segments of passion fruit and some passion fruit pulp to decorate.

NOTES

* You can use shop-bought passion fruit purée, or you can make your own by scooping out 10–15 passion fruit, removing the seeds and blitzing the liquid until smooth.

FUNFETTI CHEESECAKE

I love all things sprinkles and use them at every opportunity I can – as you will probably know if you have seen my bakes before. They bring a pop of colour, they're fun and they just help jazz things up in such a simple way. This delicious Funfetti Cheesecake recipe is so incredibly delicious and easy to make and it's the sort of dessert you can whip up for any day of the week, or for a nice meal with friends. I always, always, always recommend using cake decorating sprinkles rather than supermarket-own so that they're super bright.

SERVES: 12

PREP: 30 minutes
SET: 5–6+ hours
DECORATE: 20 minutes
LASTS: 3+ days,
in the fridge

300g digestive biscuits
100g unsalted butter, melted

Filling

500g full-fat soft cheese
100g icing sugar
2 tsp vanilla extract
300ml double cream
50–100g funfetti sprinkles

Decoration

150ml double cream
2 tbsp icing sugar
Funfetti sprinkles

Blitz the biscuits to a fine crumb in a food processor or crush in a bowl with a rolling pin. Add the melted butter and mix together. Press into the base of a 20cm springform cake tin.

Filling

In a large bowl, whisk the soft cheese, icing sugar and vanilla extract together until combined. Pour in the double cream and whisk until thickened. Alternatively, whisk the double cream in a separate bowl and then fold through the cheesecake mixture.

Fold through the funfetti sprinkles and then spread the mixture over the biscuit base. Set in the fridge for at least 5–6 hours or overnight.

Decoration

Remove the cheesecake from the tin and place on a serving plate. Whip the double cream and icing sugar together until soft peaks form and pipe onto the cheesecake. Decorate with funfetti sprinkles.

NOTES
- Cake decorating sprinkles are always best, as some supermarket sprinkles may leak their colour.
- You can flavour the cheesecake however you like – try 1–2 teaspoons of lemon, orange, coffee or almond extract.

RUM AND RAISIN CHEESECAKE

When you put rum and raisins together you get something spectacular. It's such a classic flavour combination that I simply had to include this recipe because I know you will all want to make it too. I pre-soak the raisins in rum to get as much flavour into them as possible. The base is baked slightly to help stop the cheesecake filling soaking in, but this doesn't take long. You'll be able to throw the filling together in no time, so the only hard part is waiting for the cheesecake to set – but as with any cheesecake, it's 100% worth the wait, I promise.

SERVES: 12

PREP: 2+ hours
BAKE: 50 minutes
COOL: 2 hours
SET: 5–6+ hours
LASTS: 3+ days,
in the fridge

150g raisins
100ml rum
300g digestive biscuits
100g unsalted butter, melted

Filling

600g full-fat soft cheese
175g caster sugar
30g plain flour
1 tsp vanilla extract
3 eggs
150ml soured cream

Add the raisins to a bowl and pour over the rum. For best results do this the night before making the cheesecake, or for at least 2 hours.

Preheat the oven to 220°C/200°C fan and grab a 20cm springform cake tin.

Blitz the biscuits to a fine crumb in a food processor or crush in a bowl with a rolling pin. Add the melted butter and mix together. Press into the base of the tin and bake in the oven for 10 minutes.

Filling

In a bowl, mix the soft cheese to loosen it. Add the sugar and flour and beat until combined. Add the vanilla extract, eggs and soured cream and beat again until combined. Fold through the rum-soaked raisins and any leftover rum. Pour the mixture over the baked base.

Bake in the oven for 10 minutes, then reduce the temperature to 110°C/90°C fan and bake for a further 30 minutes. Leave to cool in the oven with the door ajar for 2 hours, then chill for at least 5–6 hours, preferably overnight. Once set, remove from the tin carefully and serve with a dollop of whipped cream if you fancy.

NOTES

- If you want to prevent any cracking in the cheesecake, you can bake it in a bain-marie: grab a roasting tray larger than your cheesecake tin and fill it with 2.5cm hot water. Wrap the base and sides of the cheesecake tin in foil, then fill as above. The foil is to prevent the water getting into the cheesecake. Place the cheesecake in the roasting tray and bake as above.

CUSTARD SLICE

A custard slice is an absolute classic, and I can never just have a single piece. I would buy one on a daily basis if I could, so when you can make an entire batch at home much more easily than you think, it's a little dangerous. Yes, I know, shop-bought pastry... but I don't care. If you want to make something delicious quickly, shortcut items make it possible. The custard is so easy to whip up, with the perfect balance of sweetness. The gelatine helps set the custard to a gorgeous texture, but you can use a vegetarian alternative if you need to.

MAKES: 12

PREP: 45 minutes
BAKE: 20 minutes
COOL: 30 minutes
SET: 3–4+ hours
LASTS: 3+ days, in the fridge

400g puff pastry
Plain flour, for dusting

Custard

2 tsp vanilla extract
125g caster sugar
4 egg yolks
100g cornflour
725ml whole milk
12g powdered gelatine
2 tbsp boiling water
Icing sugar, for dusting

Preheat the oven to 220°C/200°C fan and get four baking trays. (If you only have two, you'll just need to bake one sheet of pastry at a time.)

Split the puff pastry into two 200g pieces. On a lightly floured work surface, roll out the pastry into two 20cm squares. Place a piece of parchment paper onto a baking tray and put a square of puff pastry on top. Top the pastry with a second piece of parchment paper and then top with a second baking tray – the pastry should be sandwiched between two sheets of parchment paper and trays. Bake in the oven for 20 minutes. Remove the top baking tray and parchment paper and leave to cool on the bottom tray.

Custard

Add the vanilla extract, sugar, egg yolks and cornflour to a large pan. Whisk to start to combine, then slowly add the milk and whisk until the mixture is smooth. Heat the mixture over a low heat to dissolve the sugar, whisking constantly. Once dissolved, increase the heat and boil to thicken, whisking constantly. Once the mixture has thickened, remove from the heat. Dissolve the gelatine in the boiling water, then beat into the custard.

Assembly

Line the bottom and sides of a 20cm square tin with parchment paper. Add one of the sheets of pastry to the tin. Pour the custard over the top, then top with the second sheet of pastry. Set the custard slices in the fridge for at least 3–4 hours, or overnight if possible. Dust with icing sugar before serving.

NOTES

* You want the custard to be extremely thick to set properly, so don't be scared you have taken it too far.

JAM ROLY-POLY

When I was younger, I always loved anything that involved jam and custard, even if it was just those two things on their own. So whenever I have the chance to enjoy some nostalgia with a chunk of jam roly-poly absolutely doused in custard, I always say yes. It's one of those puddings that I know you will all want to keep going back to over and over, just like me. If you've never made jam roly-poly before, the method of baking it may sound a little odd but trust me, it works. You honestly can't beat a classic pud like this.

SERVES: 8–10

PREP: 30 minutes
BAKE: 1 hour
COOL: 1 hour
LASTS: 3+ days,
in the fridge

20g unsalted butter, for greasing
225g self-raising flour
15g caster sugar
1 tsp vanilla extract
100g suet
100–150ml whole milk
250g raspberry jam

Preheat the oven to 180°C/160°C fan and place a large roasting tray filled with water at the bottom of the oven. Get a large piece of foil and place a slightly smaller piece of parchment paper in the middle of the foil. Grease the baking parchment with the butter. Set aside for now.

Pulse the flour, sugar, vanilla extract and suet together in a food processor, and slowly pour in the milk until it combines and comes together. Alternatively, you can rub the ingredients together in a bowl. On a floured work surface, roll out the mixture into a large square. Spread the jam onto the sponge, leaving a gap at one end. Roll the sponge up tightly and leave the 'seal' on the bottom. Place the rolled-up sponge on the greased parchment paper. Tightly roll the foil/parchment around the roly-poly but leave a small gap so the roly-poly has space to grow while it bakes. Bake in the oven on the shelf above the roasting tray for 1 hour. Leave to cool for 10 minutes before unwrapping and leaving to cool further.

NOTES

- *I love serving my Jam Roly-Poly with custard – the best of the best.*
- *You can use any flavour jam you prefer.*
- *You can use classic suet, or a vegetarian suet like I do.*

SPOTTED DICK

Another absolute retro classic that you will probably want to bake every day because 1) it's really just so easy to make the mixture, 2) you can leave the pud steaming while you make your dinner and 3) it's totally scrumptious. I mix all the ingredients together in a bowl, then pour it into my pudding container and go! It's such a fruity, traditional sponge, which is amazing served with custard, and will entertain the taste buds of everyone in the family!

SERVES: 6–8

PREP: 30 minutes
COOK: 1 hour 40 minutes
COOL: 10 minutes
LASTS: 3+ days,
at room temperature

275g self-raising flour
125g suet, shredded
175g currants
100g caster sugar
Zest of 1 lemon (optional)
Zest of 1 orange (optional)
150–175ml whole milk

In bowl, briefly combine the flour, suet, currants, sugar, lemon and orange zests. Slowly pour in the milk, mixing as you go, until you have a thick mixture. Pour the mixture into a 1.5-litre pudding mould.

Grab a square of foil and top with a square of parchment paper. Fold in the middle and then fold back so you have a flap for growing room. Secure this around the pudding mould with a large elastic band or string and place the pudding into a large pan filled with 2.5–5cm of water. The water should come up the sides of the pudding, but not reach the top. Put the lid on the pan, then simmer and steam the pudding for 1 hour 40 minutes, keeping an eye on the water level so it doesn't run dry. Remove from the pan carefully and leave to cool for 10 minutes before removing the pudding from the mould.

NOTES

* This pudding is best served fresh with a glug of custard for a delicious everyday dessert.
* The citrus flavouring is optional.
* You can use vegetarian or classic suet.

GIANT SKILLET BROWNIE

If I put this in front of you, I'm sure that you would struggle to say no to digging in, which is why it's one of the top recipes on my blog. There is something so moreish and wonderful about a warm gooey brownie, so when you make it a delicious sharing dessert which you could bake daily, it's even better. Imagine this after work on a Friday, just before the weekend starts, topped with your favourite ice cream and a drizzle of caramel. Heaven in every single bite, I promise.

SERVES: 8–10

PREP: 20 minutes
BAKE: 25–30 minutes
COOL: 15 minutes
LASTS: 3+ days,
at room temperature
(but best served
fresh)

200g dark chocolate
200g unsalted butter
275g caster sugar or soft light brown sugar
4 eggs
100g plain flour
50g cocoa powder
½ tsp sea salt
150g white chocolate chips
150g milk chocolate chips

To Serve

Vanilla ice cream
Caramel sauce (see page 77)

Preheat the oven to 180°C/160°C fan and grab a 25cm ovenproof skillet (frying pan).

In a heatproof bowl, break up the dark chocolate into pieces and add the butter. Melt together in the microwave in shorts bursts or set the bowl over a pan of simmering water (bain-marie) until smooth. Leave to cool for 5 minutes.

In a separate bowl, whisk the sugar and eggs together on a high speed until doubled in volume and mousse-like. The whisk should leave a trail in the mixture. Fold in the cooled chocolate mixture, then fold through the flour, cocoa powder and sea salt. Finally, fold through the chocolate chips. Pour the mixture into the skillet.

Bake in the oven for 25–30 minutes, or until there is an ever so slight wobble in the middle. Leave to cool for 15 minutes. Top with scoops of ice cream and caramel sauce and serve while warm and gooey.

NOTES

* You can add 100g caramel sauce to the middle of the skillet brownie by pouring half of the brownie mix in, topping with the caramel and then covering with the remaining brownie mixture.

* Try adding fruit for an extra flavour – 200g raspberries or cherries work perfectly.

CHOCOLATE ORANGE TRIFLE

This fan favourite trifle is probably quite far away from the traditional version, but that's fine as I'm here to introduce new and delicious ideas to inspire you to create your own! Also, I am just chocolate orange obsessed. This trifle features all of my favourite things with a chocolate orange custard, a whipped cream, Swiss roll and, of course, as much chocolate orange chocolate as possible. It's simple, easy to make and fun!

SERVES: 10

PREP: 30 minutes
SET: 1 hour
DECORATE: 30 minutes
LASTS: 2+ days,
in the fridge

500ml ready-made custard
150g chocolate orange chocolate

Cream

600ml double cream
Zest of 1 orange
2 tbsp icing sugar
2 tbsp Cointreau

Cake

1 x 350–450g chocolate Swiss roll
Juice of 1 orange
3–4 tbsp Cointreau

Filling / Decoration

2 x 300g tins mandarin segments
Chocolate orange chocolate
Grated chocolate
Orange zest

Add the custard to a small pan and heat over a low heat until starting to warm through. Add the chocolate to the custard and stir until melted. Leave to cool for 5 minutes.

Cream

In a large bowl, whisk the cream, orange zest, icing sugar and Cointreau until soft peaks form.

Cake

Slice the chocolate Swiss roll into 1–2cm slices. Drizzle over the orange juice and Cointreau.

Assembly

Place half of the Swiss roll over the base of the trifle bowl. Pour over half of the chocolate orange custard. Add segments of mandarin, then add the remaining Swiss roll and custard. Spread over the whipped orange cream and decorate with chocolate orange chocolate segments, grated chocolate and orange zest. Set the trifle for 1 hour in the fridge.

NOTES

- If you want a layer of jelly, I'd recommend dissolving 1 packet of orange jelly cubes in 250ml boiling water, then adding 250ml cold water. Pour this over the first layer of Swiss roll and let it set before continuing as in the recipe above.

- You can use chocolate sponge if you prefer, you will need about 400g.

LEMON BLUEBERRY TRIFLE

We can argue over and over about the best part of a trifle, what the correct order is and so on, but let's be honest, it all tastes DELICIOUS. For me, trifles are something you can make for a special occasion, but you can also whip up for Sunday lunch, for dessert or just because you fancy one. Lemon and blueberries are such a wonderful fresh flavour combination, perfect for enjoying in summer months or to finish off a BBQ.

SERVES: 10

PREP: 30 minutes
SET: 4–5 hours
DECORATE: 30 minutes
LASTS: 2+ days,
in the fridge

1 packet of lemon jelly cubes
250ml boiling water
250ml cold water
200g sponge fingers
100ml limoncello
500ml ready-made custard
400g blueberries
400g blueberry jam
400g lemon curd

Cream

600ml double cream
2 tbsp icing sugar
Zest of 2 lemons

Add the lemon jelly cubes to a large jug and pour over the boiling water. Whisk together to melt the jelly cubes. Pour in the cold water and whisk again.

In a trifle bowl, add half of the sponge fingers and drizzle over half the limoncello.

Pour the jelly mix over the sponge fingers. Leave to set for 3–4 hours in the fridge.

Once the jelly has set, pour over the custard. Sprinkle over half the blueberries. Carefully pour and spread the blueberry jam over the top. Add the remaining sponge fingers and drizzle over the rest of the limoncello. Spread on the lemon curd.

Cream

In a bowl, whip the double cream with the icing sugar and dollop this on top of the trifle. Sprinkle over some lemon zest and the remaining blueberries. Leave to set for a minimum of 1 hour in the fridge.

NOTES

- You can layer the trifle in any way you want – there are no rules!

- If you want an alcohol-free trifle, you can leave out the limoncello, or swap it for elderflower cordial for a different flavour.

TIRAMISU

To say tiramisu is one of the most highly requested recipes I have ever had is an understatement. It's the sort of dessert that makes all the coffee lovers go 'Ooooh' when they see it on a menu, and it's always popular if someone brings a ready-made one home from the shop. But do you know what? Making it at home makes it even better, and a hundred times more delicious. It's indulgent but so light and airy that you'll want to eat half the tray yourself – and I wouldn't judge you because I would do exactly the same thing! It's so easy to put together despite the longer list of ingredients and it's worth every moment of making it.

SERVES: 8

PREP: 30 minutes
SET: 5+ hours
DECORATE: 10 minutes
LASTS: 2+ days,
in the fridge

2 tbsp strong instant coffee
250ml boiling water
75ml coffee liqueur (I use Kahlua)
3 egg yolks
100g caster sugar
250g mascarpone
1 tsp vanilla extract
3 egg whites
200g sponge fingers
10g cocoa powder, for dusting

Add the instant coffee, boiling water and coffee liqueur to a bowl, and mix to dissolve the coffee. Leave to cool.

Add the egg yolks and sugar to the bowl of a stand mixer and whisk for 8–10 minutes until thickened and pale. Add the mascarpone and vanilla extract to the bowl and beat together until smooth. In a separate bowl, add the egg whites and whisk until stiff peaks form. Add half of the mascarpone mixture to the bowl and fold through carefully. Once combined, add the other half and fold through again.

Dip half of the sponge fingers into the coffee mixture and add a layer to the bottom of a 23 x 15cm dish. Spread over half of the cream mixture. Dip the other half of the sponge fingers in the coffee mixture and add another layer on top of the cream. Add on the second half of the cream mixture. Place the tiramisu in the fridge for at least 5 hours, or overnight. Dust the top lightly with the cocoa powder and serve.

NOTES

- You can use coffee from a coffee machine if you have one – you just need 250ml strong coffee.

- To make this alcohol-free, leave out the coffee liqueur and increase the amount of coffee to make up the difference in liquid.

LEMON CURD MOUSSE

Sometimes you need a dessert that you can prepare quickly when you are craving something sweet, or you suddenly have guests, and this fan favourite is exactly that. A simple combination of lemon curd and cream whipped together is an incredible way of creating something delightful and, of course, you can top and decorate it how you fancy. I always love adding a dollop of whipped cream, some extra lemon curd (because why on earth not?) and some blueberries.

MAKES: 8–10

PREP: 15 minutes
CHILL: 1 hour
DECORATE: 15 minutes
LASTS: 3+ days,
in the fridge

200g lemon curd
600ml double cream

Decoration

150ml double cream
2 tbsp icing sugar
100g lemon curd
100g blueberries
Lemon zest

In a large bowl, whisk the lemon curd and double cream together until soft peaks form. Pipe or spoon the mixture into 8–10 glasses and chill for 1 hour.

In a large bowl, whip the double cream and icing sugar together until soft peaks form. Transfer to a piping bag with the piping nozzle of your choice fitted and pipe over the mousses. Add a spoonful of lemon curd, and sprinkle over the blueberries and lemon zest.

NOTES

- If you want the mousse a bit sweeter and less tart, add 75g icing sugar to the cream and whip that in.

- You can use any fruit curd you like to make other flavours, such as passion fruit.

COOKIE DOUGH ICE CREAM

I don't know about you, but I would happily eat ice cream every single day of the year and not complain. I don't know why I adore it so much, other than it being absolutely delicious and so incredibly easy to make yourself... So yeah, maybe that's why! I have had endless requests over the years to create this Cookie Dough Ice Cream because it is one of the best flavours in the world, so here you go. I bake the flour in the cookie dough briefly to kill off any germs, and then it's super, super easy. I add chocolate chips to my cookie dough, and some baked crunchy cookies, and mix them into a super-easy vanilla ice cream mixture. YUMMY.

SERVES: 8–10

PREP: 30 minutes
BAKE: 5 minutes
COOL: 5 minutes
FREEZE: 2+ hours
LASTS: 3+ days,
in the freezer

175g plain flour
125g unsalted butter, at room
    temperature
160g soft light brown sugar
1 tsp vanilla extract
30ml whole milk
150g chocolate of your choice,
    finely chopped

Preheat the oven to 200°C/180°C fan and line a large baking tray with parchment paper.

Sprinkle the flour evenly over the tray and bake in the oven for 5 minutes. Transfer to a bowl and leave to cool for 5 minutes.

In a separate bowl, beat the butter and sugar together until combined. Add the baked flour, vanilla extract, milk and chocolate.

Beat to form a cookie dough. Roll into balls of cookie dough about 2 teaspoons-worth in size.

Ice Cream

In a separate bowl, whisk the double cream, condensed milk and vanilla extract together until starting to thicken. Layer the mixture into a large container or 900g loaf tin with the cookie dough balls and chopped cookies. Freeze until solid.

Ice Cream

600ml double cream
397g tin condensed milk
1 tsp vanilla extract
100g baked cookies, chopped
    (optional)

NOTES

- You can make the ice cream chocolate-flavoured by whisking in 150g chocolate spread, or 50g cocoa powder.

- The baked cookies are optional but bring a delicious crunchy element to the ice cream.

Comfort Food

MACARONI CHEESE

When I think of comfort, I often think of cheese. A macaroni cheese like this fan favourite is always just so warming and comforting, and so easy to make. Put away those jars of cheese sauce and give it a go, because honestly, it's worth it. Not only does my Macaroni Cheese please the adults, but it's the sort of dish that the entire family will happily enjoy.

SERVES: 4–6

PREP: 30 minutes
BAKE: 25 minutes
LASTS: 2+ days in the fridge (but best served fresh)

350g macaroni
200g bacon lardons
50g mature Cheddar cheese, grated
75g breadcrumbs, made from stale bread

Sauce

35g unsalted butter
35g plain flour
1 tsp mustard powder
2 garlic cloves, finely chopped
565ml whole milk
Salt and pepper
300g mature Cheddar cheese, grated
50g Parmesan, grated

Cook the macaroni for 2 minutes less than the packet instructions. Drain and set aside.

Cook the bacon lardons in a dry pan over a medium-high heat until the bacon is cooked through and crispy.

Sauce

Melt the butter and flour in a medium pan over a low heat, mixing together. Once melted, increase the heat and add the mustard powder and garlic. Fry, stirring well, for 1–2 minutes to cook out the flour. Gradually add the milk, whisking well – I find it best to add small amounts at first to prevent a lumpy sauce. Once you have added all the milk, continue to simmer for about 5 minutes, stirring constantly. Season well with salt and pepper. Add the Cheddar and Parmesan and stir in and melt off the heat.

Preheat the oven to 200°C/180°C fan.

Add the cooked bacon lardons to the bottom of a large baking dish, then add the macaroni on top. Pour over the cheese sauce, then stir together. Sprinkle over the remaining Cheddar, then add the breadcrumbs. Bake in the oven for 25 minutes until the top is golden and bubbling.

NOTES

- *Depending on how much liquid fat is produced, you can use the bacon fat instead of the butter in the sauce if you want some extra flavour.*

- *You can use less mature cheese if you prefer – any Cheddar works well.*

- *If you want a little kick to your cheese sauce, try adding 1 teaspoon of paprika.*

TOAD IN THE HOLE

When it's a slightly cold and autumnal day I always crave something like this... it's the definition of cosy food. Toad In The Hole is the sort of dish that you probably grew up with – I certainly did. It always looks so impressive, even though it's incredibly easy to make. The Yorkshire pudding batter is simple to mix up, and then you just whack everything else together. The gravy is a tasty addition because I think you MUST have gravy with this Toad In The Hole – it's a sin not to! This would be delicious served with some green veg, and my Ultimate Roast Potatoes on page 194.

SERVES: 6

PREP: 30 minutes
COOK: 40–45 minutes
LASTS: Best served fresh

100g plain flour
2 eggs
150ml whole milk
8–10 sausages
2 onions, sliced
2 tbsp olive oil
Salt and pepper
2 garlic cloves, crushed

Gravy

25g unsalted butter
1 onion, finely chopped
2 garlic cloves, crushed
2 tbsp plain flour
1 vegetable stock cube
300ml boiling water
Salt and pepper

Preheat the oven to 220°C/200°C fan and get a large baking or roasting tray.

In a large bowl, whisk the flour, eggs and milk together until smooth. Add the sausages and sliced onion to the baking tray and drizzle over the olive oil. Roast the sausages and onions for 15 minutes. Sprinkle on the salt and pepper, and the crushed garlic. Pour over the batter and cook for a further 25–30 minutes, or until the sausages are cooked through.

Gravy

While the Toad In The Hole is cooking, make the gravy. Add the butter to a large pan and heat so it starts to bubble. Add the onion and fry for a few minutes to start to soften. Add the garlic and flour and cook for a couple of minutes, stirring often so that the flour doesn't catch. Dissolve the stock cube in the boiling water, then slowly pour the stock into the pan, whisking well, until all of the liquid has been added. Continue to cook over a medium heat until the gravy has thickened to your liking. Season with salt and pepper. Serve the Toad In The Hole immediately with the gravy.

NOTES

- *Feel free to flavour your gravy with any of the following:*
  - *1 tbsp Worcestershire sauce*
  - *1 tbsp English or wholegrain mustard*
  - *½ tsp dried thyme, ½ tsp dried sage and ½ tsp dried rosemary.*

- *If you want to make this vegetarian, just use vegetarian sausages.*

- *You can use any flavour stock for the gravy.*

TOMATO, RICOTTA AND SPINACH PASTA BAKE

Pasta is one of my favourite things to eat, as you enjoy it in so many different ways.
You have your classics such as Bolognese and lasagne when you want a tomato-based
sauce, but this bake is just another level of heaven. Ricotta isn't something I normally
pick up, but it works incredibly well mixed with the easy tomato sauce and the spinach.
Bake it all together for a rich and wonderful weeknight winner.

SERVES: 6

PREP: 30 minutes
COOK: 25–30 minutes
LASTS: Best served
fresh

300g pasta of your choice
150g spinach
500g ricotta
35g Parmesan
3 garlic cloves, crushed
350g mozzarella, grated
Salt and pepper

Sauce

600ml passata
3 garlic cloves, finely chopped
1 tsp onion powder
1 tsp garlic powder
2 tsp mixed herbs
1 tsp chilli flakes
Salt and pepper

Preheat the oven to 200°C/180°C fan.

Cook the pasta for 2 minutes less than the packet instructions.
Drain and set aside.

Cook the spinach in a large pan until wilted. Remove from the pan.

In a large bowl, mix the ricotta, Parmesan, garlic, cooked spinach
and 150g of the mozzarella together. Season with salt and pepper,
then mix it all together to form a thick paste.

Sauce

In a separate bowl, mix the passata, garlic, onion powder, garlic
powder, mixed herbs, chilli flakes and salt and pepper together.

Add the pasta to the cheese filling and mix through. Spread onto
the bottom of a large baking dish. Pour over the tomato sauce, then
sprinkle over the remaining grated mozzarella. Bake in the oven for
25–30 minutes until the cheese is melted and golden.

NOTES

- *You can use whatever pasta you like for this – fusilli, penne, rigatoni, etc.*
- *You can use frozen spinach instead of fresh if you prefer – simply thaw
  before using.*

CHORIZO AND HALLOUMI TRAYBAKE

Chorizo is warm, spicy and packed full of flavour and this traybake is something that you can just whack together with no real prep and get on with anything else you need to do in the house while it bakes. Adding the halloumi and tomatoes at the end creates a perfect balance of flavour and texture. Serve with a salad or grab a chunk of bread – YUM!

SERVES: 6

PREP: 30 minutes
COOK: 30–35 minutes
LASTS: Best served fresh

300g new potatoes, boiled and halved
200g chorizo, cut into 2.5cm chunks
2 red onions, sliced
1 red pepper, sliced
1 tsp chilli flakes
1 tsp smoked paprika
Salt and pepper
Olive oil
200g halloumi, cut into 2.5cm chunks
200g cherry tomatoes, halved

Preheat the oven to 210°C/190°C fan and grab a large baking dish.

Add the cooked new potatoes, chorizo chunks, red onions and red pepper to the dish. Sprinkle over the chilli flakes, smoked paprika and salt and pepper. Drizzle over the olive oil and mix together briefly. Cook in the oven for 25 minutes. Remove from the oven and add the chunks of halloumi and cherry tomatoes. Grill on a high heat for 5–10 minutes until the halloumi is slightly golden and the tomatoes are tender.

NOTES

- *If you want to add any extra veg, then go for it – try mushrooms and courgettes.*

- *Switch the red onion for white, or use any other coloured pepper.*

- *You can use tinned and cooked new potatoes.*

CHEESE AND BROCCOLI BAKE

As we all know by now, I adore anything cheese flavoured. A cheese scone, cheese twist, cheese sauce, I could go on... So when I want something super comforting, I bake this beauty. It's the best side dish to almost anything you fancy, but you can even elevate it into a spectacular main pasta dish (see the Notes below). I love a mature Cheddar and Parmesan cheese sauce, flavoured with a little garlic and mustard powder to pack a punch. The gooey cheesy sauce works wonders with the broccoli, and I could happily sit and devour the entire thing on my own, although it's a great dish for sharing if you can bear it.

SERVES: 6+

PREP: 30 minutes
BAKE: 20–25 minutes
LASTS: Best served fresh

750g broccoli, broken or cut into small florets

50g Parmesan, grated

100g mature Cheddar cheese, grated

200g dried breadcrumbs

Sauce

35g unsalted butter

35g plain flour

1 tsp mustard powder

2 garlic cloves, finely chopped

Salt and pepper

500ml whole milk

300g mature Cheddar cheese, grated

50g Parmesan, grated

Preheat the oven to 210°C/190°C fan and get a large baking dish.

Bring a large pan of water to the boil, and par-boil the broccoli for a few minutes. You might need to do this in two batches. Drain and set aside.

Sauce

For the sauce, melt the butter and flour in a medium pan over a low heat, mixing together. Once melted, increase the heat and add the mustard powder, garlic, salt and pepper. Fry, stirring well, for 1–2 minutes to cook out the flour. Gradually add the milk, whisking well – I find it best to add small amounts at first to prevent a lumpy sauce. Once you have added all the milk, continue to simmer for about 5 minutes, stirring constantly. Add the Cheddar and Parmesan and stir in and melt off the heat.

Place the broccoli into a large baking dish, and then pour over the cheese sauce. Sprinkle on the extra cheese, and then add the breadcrumbs. Bake in the oven for 20–25 minutes until the top is golden and bubbling.

NOTES

- *If you want to make this into a main meal, swap out 350g of the broccoli for pasta – cook the pasta for 2 minutes less than the packet instructions.*

- *The broccoli can be swapped entirely or partly for cauliflower if you prefer.*

CHICKEN FAJITA TRAYBAKE

I love any dish full of flavour and spice – it calls to me. I want something to have a punch to it, and this traybake certainly passes the test. Amazing served as it is, or with some salad, or even whacked into a wrap for a quick lunch. I love the red onion and pepper slices with the chicken, and then you get another level of texture from the beans and rice. It's an easy throw-together dinner that I adore.

SERVES: 4+

PREP: 30 minutes
BAKE: 25–30 minutes
LASTS: Best served
fresh

1 tsp chilli powder

1 tsp smoked paprika

1 tsp ground cumin

1 tsp dried oregano

1 tsp garlic powder

1 tsp onion powder

½ tsp salt

1 red onion, sliced

1 yellow pepper, sliced

1 red pepper, sliced

400g chicken breasts, cut into chunks

2 tbsp olive oil

200g tinned black beans

200g cooked rice

10g fresh coriander, chopped

In a small bowl, mix the chilli powder, smoked paprika, ground cumin, dried oregano, garlic powder, onion powder and salt together well.

Preheat the oven to 210°C/190°C fan and grab a large roasting tray.

Add the red onion, yellow pepper, red pepper and chicken to the tray. Drizzle over the olive oil, then sprinkle over the spice mix. Stir the mix together and then bake in the oven for 20 minutes. Remove from the oven carefully and add the black beans and cooked rice. Mix everything together slightly and return to the oven for a further 5–10 minutes to continue cooking the chicken and heat up the beans and rice. Remove from the oven and sprinkle over the coriander to serve.

NOTES

- The peppers and onions can be swapped for other colours if you prefer.

- If you want a little more spice and heat, I'd recommend adding some chilli flakes, plus an extra teaspoon of chilli powder – and make it the hot one!

- To make a veggie traybake, remove the chicken and double the quantities of veg.

CHEESY GARLIC BREAD TRAYBAKE

If you don't like garlic, I don't think we can be friends. There is something about it that just calls to me, and I often like to add more than a recipe will ask for because there is just never enough. This Cheesy Garlic Bread Traybake is comfort in a bowl, and I would like to devour it all to myself, thanks. But honestly, it's great as part of any dish. Try it on the side of my Macaroni Cheese (see page 146), or even my Tomato, Ricotta and Spinach Pasta Bake (see page 150) or just because you fancy some garlic bread! I often make this and use the bread to make a toastie – levelling up toasties since 2014.

SERVES: 6-8

PREP: 30 minutes
PROVE: 1-2 hours
BAKE: 20-25 minutes
LASTS: Best served fresh

300g strong white bread flour
7g dried yeast
1 tsp salt
Pinch of sugar
30ml olive oil, plus extra for greasing
185ml warm water

Topping

50g unsalted butter, melted
5 garlic cloves, finely chopped
15g fresh parsley, finely chopped
200g mozzarella cheese, grated

Sift the flour into a large bowl, then add the yeast, salt and sugar. Mix together, then add the oil and water and start to knead the dough to bring the mixture together. Continue to knead the dough for 7-10 minutes – it will be sticky at first, but it will soon come together. The dough should be springy to the touch, and not sticky. Transfer into a lightly oiled bowl and cover the top of the bowl with clingfilm. Leave it to rise for 1-2 hours, or until doubled in size.

Preheat the oven to 220°C/200°C fan and line a large baking tray.

Topping

Once the dough has risen, turn it out onto a lightly oiled surface and press into a rectangular shape. Transfer to the tray, then press your fingers into the dough slightly to create dips. Mix the melted butter with the garlic and spread this over the bread. Bake in the oven for 10 minutes. Remove carefully, sprinkle over the parsley, then the cheese. Reduce the oven temperature to 200°C/180°C fan and return to the oven for a further 10-15 minutes. The cheese should be golden and bubbling wonderfully.

NOTES

- You can add more or less garlic depending on how garlicky you like things.
- Try 1 teaspoon of dried parsley instead of fresh if you prefer.
- The mozzarella can be swapped for Cheddar if you fancy.

ULTIMATE NACHOS

I am utterly obsessed with Nachos, and while that probably isn't the healthiest of obsessions I really don't care. Whenever I go to the cinema, whenever I just want a quick snack etc, NACHOS. However, these are the Ultimate Nachos and one of the top recipes on my blog. With a homemade salsa, guacamole and spicy mince – what more could you want?! Oh yeah, all the cheese on top. It may seem like a lot of ingredients, but honestly these nachos are so easy to put together, and 100% worth it. Either make giant layers or create multiple layers of goodness – whatever you prefer.

SERVES: 4

PREP: 1 hour
COOK: 15 minutes
LASTS: Best served fresh

Salsa

2 large tomatoes
½ small red onion
½ red chilli
15g fresh coriander
Juice of 1 lime
Salt and pepper

Guacamole

2 ripe medium avocados
½ small red onion
½ large tomato
Juice of ½ lime
Salt and pepper
Pinch of chilli flakes

Mince

250g beef mince
1 tbsp Cajun spice
Salt and pepper
2 garlic cloves, finely chopped

Salsa

Chop the tomatoes into small dice, along with the red onion. Finely chop the red chilli and coriander. Add all these to a bowl, along with the lime juice and some salt and pepper. Mix together and set aside.

Guacamole

Peel and core the avocados, then add the flesh to a bowl. Mash the avocado on its own for a bit to start to soften it and break it down. Finely chop the red onion and tomato and add to the avocado, along with the lime juice, salt and pepper and chilli flakes. Mix together until combined and relatively smooth. Set aside.

Mince

Add the beef mince to a dry frying pan over a medium heat. Break the mince down into small pieces with a spatula, and then add the Cajun spice, salt and pepper and garlic. Fry the mince until it's all browned and cooked through. Remove from the heat.

Assembly

Grab a large baking tray or dish. Add a layer of the tortilla chips, then top with the mince.

Add most of the salsa, and some jalapeños if you fancy. Sprinkle over the grated cheese.

Place the nachos under the grill in the oven for at least 4–5 minutes until the cheese has melted. Remove from the grill and dollop on the guacamole, the soured cream and remaining salsa.

Tortilla

200g tortilla chips

Jalapeños (optional)

250g mozzarella or Cheddar
  cheese, grated

Soured cream

NOTES

- *If you want to make this quicker or vegetarian, just leave out the mince.*

- *Leave out the spice if you aren't a fan or add extra if you like it spicy!*

- *You can use flavoured tortilla chips if you fancy (or if that's what you have in the cupboard).*

BERRY CRUMBLE TRAYBAKE

We all know that there is something so wonderfully comforting about a crumble. It's literally cosiness in a dish. I wanted to create a bake that you could layer into one dish, grab out of the oven as you finish your dinner and then serve warm with some custard, cream or ice cream; or anything you fancy. Perfect everyday comfort food.

SERVES: 8+

PREP: 30 minutes
BAKE: 40–50 minutes
COOL: 10 minutes
LASTS: 2–3 days, at room temperature (but best served fresh)

120g plain flour
60g caster sugar
60g unsalted butter

Berries

250g frozen berries, such as strawberries, raspberries, blackberries, blueberries or cherries
50g caster sugar
25g cornflour

Cake

250g unsalted butter, at room temperature
250g caster sugar
250g self-raising flour
½ tsp ground ginger
½ tsp ground cinnamon
4 eggs
50ml whole milk

Add the flour, sugar and butter to a bowl and rub together with your fingertips until the mixture resembles breadcrumbs. Set aside.

Berries

Add the berries to a medium pan over a medium heat and cook for a few minutes to start to soften. Add the sugar and cornflour and mix. Simmer for 5 minutes, then remove from the heat.

Cake

Preheat the oven to 180°C/160°C fan and grab a 30 x 25cm (or other large) baking dish.

In a large bowl, beat the butter and sugar together until creamy. Add the flour, ginger, cinnamon, eggs and milk and beat until smooth. Pour half of the cake mixture into the baking dish and level out. Pour the berries on top and spread. Add the remaining cake mixture, then sprinkle over the crumble.

Bake in the oven for 40–50 minutes. Leave to cool for 10 minutes, then serve warm with custard or a glug of double cream.

NOTES

- I used a mixed bag of summer berries from the freezer aisle, but you can use any berries you like.

- You can use fresh berries, but they will only need to cook for about 2 minutes as they will be much softer.

- You can cool the traybake and enjoy cold as well – it's just as delicious.

JAMMY COCONUT TRAYBAKE

Now we all know and love the jam and coconut combination, right? It's just such a simple, retro pairing – perfect for when you fancy a taste of nostalgia. I love the flavour of coconut, and it really packs a punch when you add desiccated coconut to a basic sponge. Top it with your favourite jam – I tend to use raspberry – and sprinkle a little extra coconut flavour on top. A simple everyday bake that will bring you cosy comfort no matter the time of year.

SERVES: 8+

PREP: 30 minutes
BAKE: 45–50 minutes
COOL: 10 minutes
LASTS: 2–3 days, at room temperature (but best served fresh)

275g unsalted butter,
   at room temperature
275g caster sugar
275g self-raising flour
5 eggs
100g desiccated coconut
1 tsp vanilla extract
450g jam of your choice
50g desiccated coconut
Custard, to serve

Preheat the oven to 180°C/160°C fan and grab a 30 x 25cm (or other large) baking dish.

In a large bowl, beat the butter and sugar together until creamy. Add the flour, eggs, desiccated coconut and vanilla extract and beat until smooth. Pour into the baking dish. Bake in the oven for 45–50 minutes. Leave to cool fully.

Once cooled, spread the jam over the top, and sprinkle over the desiccated coconut.

NOTES

- *This bake is amazing served with custard – but it's wonderful on its own too.*
- *This bake freezes really well for 3+ months in a freezerproof container.*

WARM PEACH AND ALMOND CAKE

There is just something so tasty about the combination of peach and almond. The sweetness of the peaches and the delicious nuttiness from the almonds merge together to create something utterly spectacular. It's a deliciously simple bake, but sometimes simple is best. Pure comfort in a bowl.

SERVES: 8+

PREP: 30 minutes
BAKE: 45–50 minutes
COOL: 10 minutes
LASTS: 2–3 days, at room temperature (but best served fresh)

225g unsalted butter, at room temperature
225g caster sugar
225g self-raising flour
225g ground almonds
4 eggs
400g tinned peach slices, syrup reserved (optional)
75g flaked almonds
Custard, to serve

Preheat the oven to 180°C/160°C fan and grab a 30 x 25cm (or other large) baking dish.

In a large bowl, beat the butter and sugar and together until creamy. Add the flour, ground almonds and eggs and beat until smooth. Pour into the baking dish. Top with the peaches, then sprinkle over the flaked almonds. Bake in the oven for 45–50 minutes.

If you have the syrup from the tin of peaches, brush some of this over the top to let it soak in.

Leave to cool for 10 minutes, then serve warm with custard.

NOTES

- *I used tinned peaches because they are available all year round. You can use sliced fresh peaches.*
- *The peaches can be swapped for other tinned fruit really easily!*
- *You can reheat the bake in the oven at 180°C/160°C fan for about 20 minutes.*

CHOCOLATE SCHOOL CAKE AND CUSTARD

Sometimes, you simply can't beat a classic, especially when it comes to everyday baking. A School Cake is one of the best cult recipes (and blog favourites), and the chocolate version? Equally as delightful. The nostalgia I get from eating a giant chunk of this cake just can't be beaten, especially when it's doused in homemade chocolate custard. A layer of chocolate icing that's so easy to make, with a little dash of sprinkles just elevates it even more and makes it perfect for a party or other celebration.

SERVES: 15

PREP: 30 minutes
BAKE: 45–50 minutes
COOL: 1 hour
DECORATE: 30 minutes
LASTS: 3+ days, at room temperature (custard best served fresh)

400g unsalted butter, at room temperature
400g caster sugar
8 eggs
325g self-raising flour
75g cocoa powder
1 tsp vanilla extract

Icing

400g icing sugar
50g cocoa powder
4–5 tbsp water
Chocolate sprinkles

Custard

4 egg yolks
30g caster sugar
30g plain flour
300ml whole milk
1 tsp vanilla extract
50g milk chocolate
50g dark chocolate

Preheat the oven to 180°C/160°C fan and line a 23 x 33cm traybake tin with parchment paper.

In a large bowl, beat the butter and sugar together until light and fluffy. Add the eggs, flour, cocoa powder and vanilla extract and beat again. Pour the mixture into the tin and bake in the oven for 45–50 minutes. Leave to cool fully in the tin.

Icing

Add the icing sugar and cocoa powder to a medium bowl, then gradually add the water, mixing well until a thick paste is formed. Carefully spread the icing over the cake. Sprinkle over some chocolate sprinkles to decorate.

Custard

Add the egg yolks, sugar and flour to a large pan and whisk. Start to heat the mixture over a low heat. Slowly pour in the milk, while whisking, then add the vanilla extract. While whisking continuously, heat the mixture to a simmer and let it simmer for several minutes until it starts to thicken. Add the milk and dark chocolate and let this melt while whisking. Continue to heat until the custard has reached your desired consistency. Serve the cake with the custard.

NOTES

- For a cheat's custard, buy a pot of ready-made custard, add it to a pan with 150g chocolate and melt together until smooth.

- You can make the sponge vanilla-flavoured by replacing the cocoa powder with extra self-raising flour and adding another teaspoon of vanilla extract.

BREAD AND BUTTER PUDDING

When it comes to the classics, as with the others in this book, you'll want to devour every little crumb. A Jammy Coconut Traybake (see page 166), Spotted Dick (see page 130) or even Chocolate School Cake and Custard (see page 173) are all delightful. But Bread and Butter Pudding? It's totally delicious and it even uses up stale bread! As a child I couldn't understand the concept of bread being soggy in a dish but needless to say, I was just stubborn and refused to try it, because now I love this fan and family favourite.

SERVES: 6–8

PREP: 30 minutes
BAKE: 35–40 minutes
COOL: 10 minutes
LASTS: Best served fresh

400g brioche loaf
50–100g unsalted butter
75g raisins (optional)
75g chocolate chips (optional)
4 eggs
300ml double cream
300ml whole milk
50g caster sugar
50g soft light brown sugar

Preheat the oven to 180°C/160°C fan and get a 30 x 25cm baking dish.

Slice the brioche loaf into 2cm-thick slices, then cut these into triangles. Spread a small amount of butter onto each piece of bread, and then put the bread into the dish.

Sprinkle over the raisins and chocolate chips, if using. In a jug, whisk together the eggs, double cream, milk and caster sugar. Pour the custard over the bread evenly. Chill the pudding in the fridge for 20–30 minutes before baking to let it all soak in, if you have time.

Sprinkle over the brown sugar evenly and bake in the oven for 35–40 minutes. You want it to be nice and golden on top, and perfectly stodgy.

NOTES

- Stale bread, croissants, hot cross buns, etc all work well in place of the brioche.

- The raisins and chocolate are optional, or interchangeable. You can even add mixed fruit.

- You can add flavour to the custard, try 1 teaspoon of vanilla extract, ground ginger, ground cinnamon or anything else you fancy.

STICKY TOFFEE PUDDING

Sticky Toffee Pudding is probably one of the cosiest comfort puds you can make, and it's a personal and fan favourite. When it's served fresh, warm and gooey with a giant dollop of ice cream, I am in absolute heaven. There is just something about a classic everyday dessert that gets me, and I would happily eat this every day. Is it the best of the best? Oh yes.

SERVES: 10

PREP: 50 minutes
BAKE: 35–40 minutes
LASTS: 2+ days,
in the fridge

175g dates, stones removed
175ml boiling water
75g unsalted butter, at room
   temperature
175g soft dark brown sugar
250g self-raising flour
1 tsp baking powder
1 tsp bicarbonate of soda
75g black treacle
3 eggs
125ml whole milk

Sauce

75g unsalted butter
75g soft dark brown sugar
2 tbsp black treacle
1 tsp vanilla extract
150ml double cream

Chop the dates as finely as possible, put into a bowl and cover with the boiling water. Leave to soak for 20 minutes before blending to a smooth mixture in a food processor.

Preheat the oven to 180°C/160°C fan and get a 30 x 20cm baking dish ready.

In a large bowl, beat the butter, sugar, flour, baking powder, bicarbonate of soda, black treacle and eggs until combined. Add the blended date mixture and the milk and mix until well combined. Pour into the dish and bake in the oven for 35–40 minutes, or until a skewer inserted into the middle comes out clean.

Sauce

While the pudding is baking, make the sauce. Add all the sauce ingredients to a large pan and stir over a low heat until the sugar has dissolved, and the butter has melted. Bring the sauce to the boil and stir for 1–2 minutes until it has thickened. Pour half of the sauce over the baked pudding and use the rest to serve alongside.

NOTES

- *The pudding is best served fresh, but it can be reheated in the oven. The sauce can also last for 3+ days in the fridge but does thicken as it gets cold.*

- *You cannot taste the dates in the recipe, they just enhance the toffee flavour as they are blended. Please do not omit them, even if you hate them.*

- *The soft dark brown sugar can be substituted for soft light brown sugar, and you can use golden syrup instead of black treacle.*

Savoury and Breads

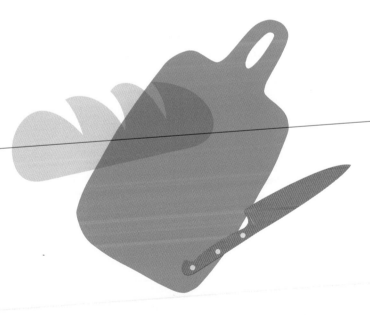

CHEESE AND ONION 'SAUSAGE' ROLLS

These delicious parcels of cheese and onion make a lovely veggie alternative to sausage rolls, and I just can't get enough of them. I scoff these as a mid-afternoon snack, as part of a 'picky tea' or even just because. Cheese and onion is an iconic flavour combination across the world, mainly because of crisps, but they are just so good together! Add pastry, some spices and you have something for the whole family to enjoy.

MAKES: 16

PREP: 30 minutes
BAKE: 20 minutes
COOL: 10 minutes
LASTS: 3+ days, in the fridge (but best served fresh)

2 large potatoes, peeled and chopped
2 large white onions, chopped
200g extra mature Cheddar cheese, grated
50g unsalted butter
1 tsp mustard powder
Salt and pepper
1 tsp dried thyme
½ tsp cayenne pepper
2 x sheets of puff pastry
Plain flour, for dusting
1 egg, beaten

Preheat the oven to 210°C/190°C fan and line 2–3 large baking trays with parchment paper.

Boil the potatoes in a large pan until cooked through, then drain and leave to cool for 5 minutes. Once the potatoes have cooled slightly, add them to a large bowl and mash. Add the onions, Cheddar, butter, mustard powder, salt and pepper, thyme and cayenne pepper. Mix until combined.

Unroll the two sheets of puff pastry onto a lightly floured surface. Cut each sheet into eight squares. Divide the potato mixture between the 16 squares of pastry, dolloping onto one side of the square and leaving a gap around the edge. Fold the pastry squares over to seal in the filling, and seal with a fork, or press down firmly. Brush the tops with beaten egg, then bake in the oven for 20 minutes until golden. Leave to cool for 5–10 minutes, then enjoy.

NOTES

- You can bake this like the Sausage Plait on page 96 to make a giant roll, follow the same baking time and pastry quantities.

- Try sprinkling over a little grated Parmesan before baking to give an extra hint of cheese, like in my Pizza Pockets recipe on page 184.

- These freeze really well once baked and reheat perfectly in an oven preheated to 190°C/170°C fan.

PIZZA POCKETS

Pizza is the sort of meal that I don't think I could ever get bored of. There are so many flavour combinations for something different every day of the week, however, sometimes I feel like pizza is a bit too much for a snack. Therefore, when you want something a little different to share or have fun making, these pizza pockets are the one. They are little parcels of heaven, with a deliciously cheesy and tomatoey filling, with pepperoni and a smidge of basil.

MAKES: 12

PREP: 30 minutes
BAKE: 18–22 minutes
COOL: 10 minutes
LASTS: 3+ days, in the fridge (but best served fresh)

Sauce

3 tbsp tomato purée
1 tsp onion powder
1 tsp garlic powder
1 tsp Italian mixed herbs
1 tsp chilli flakes
Salt and pepper
2 tbsp water

Pockets

2 x sheets of puff pastry
Plain flour, for dusting
60g pepperoni pieces
12 fresh basil leaves
200g mozzarella, grated
2 tsp dried oregano
25g Parmesan

Sauce

Add the tomato purée, onion powder, garlic powder, Italian mixed herbs, chilli flakes, salt and pepper and water to a bowl and mix together to make a paste.

Pockets

Preheat the oven to 220°C/200°C fan and line two large baking trays with parchment paper.

Unroll the puff pastry sheets onto a lightly floured surface and cut each one into six squares to make 12 in total. Divide the pizza sauce between the pastry squares and spread slightly. Add a few pieces of pepperoni to each square, then add a basil leaf. Sprinkle over the mozzarella. Fold the squares over and seal with a fork to make the pockets. Sprinkle over the dried oregano and Parmesan.

Bake in the oven for 18–22 minutes until golden.

NOTES

- You can swap the filling flavours for your favourite pizza toppings. Just stick to similar quantities so your pockets still seal shut.

- You can switch the puff pastry for a ready-made pizza dough if you want, but the pastry is quicker and easier!

ROAST VEGETABLE HALLOUMI SKEWERS

When I have a load of vegetables to use up, I tend to roast them for future dinners. You can then add them to pasta, enjoy alongside a roast or use them on top of a pizza. However, making deliciously marinated Roast Vegetable Halloumi Skewers with a dip? Oh, okay then. These beautiful skewers are a brilliant addition to a meal, to a BBQ, as well as a great way to use up leftovers. Honestly, they're so easy to make as well.

MAKES: 6

PREP: 20 minutes
COOK: 5–10 minutes
LASTS: Best served fresh

200g halloumi, cut into 2.5cm pieces
1 courgette, cut into 2cm pieces
1 red pepper, cut into 2cm pieces
1 yellow pepper, cut into 2cm pieces
1 red onion, cut into chunks
A drizzle of olive oil
1 tsp garlic powder
1 tsp onion powder
1 tsp mixed herbs
1 tbsp honey
1 tsp harissa paste
Salt and pepper

Dip

200g Greek yoghurt
10g fresh coriander, finely chopped
¼ cucumber, finely chopped
Salt and pepper

Grab six large metal or wooden skewers (soaked for 30 minutes). Thread the halloumi and vegetables randomly onto the skewers to make a variety of combinations.

In a small bowl, mix the olive oil, garlic powder, onion powder, mixed herbs, honey, harissa paste and salt and pepper together. Brush the mixture all over the skewers.

Preheat the grill to high, then grill the skewers for 5–10 minutes, turning often. Alternatively, cook on a griddle on the hob, or even on the BBQ.

Dip

While the skewers are cooking, throw the dip together by mixing the yoghurt, coriander, cucumber and salt and pepper together. Serve with the freshly cooked skewers.

NOTES

- You can use any vegetables you want – cherry tomatoes, mushrooms and broccoli all work well.

- You can add pieces of meat instead of the halloumi, but they may need partially cooking first.

- If you don't want to grill your skewers, you can cook them in the oven at 200ºC/180ºC fan for 15–20 minutes.

PROSCIUTTO AND ASPARAGUS BUNDLES

These little bundles of heaven are one of the easiest snacks to make, and I always want to eat the entire bunch. There is something so pleasant about the flavour combination of asparagus, tied with the saltiness of the prosciutto. Add the lemon and seasoning and you just lift the flavours even more! These are brilliant as an addition to any meal, as a snack, or even as an appetiser for a celebratory meal.

MAKES: 8

PREP: 15 minutes
BAKE: 12–15 minutes
LASTS: 3+ days, in the fridge (but best served fresh)

500g asparagus
8 slices of prosciutto
Olive oil
Salt and pepper
Zest of 1 lemon

Preheat the oven to 200°C/180°C fan and line two large baking trays with parchment paper.

Split the asparagus into eight even-sized bundles. Grab a piece of prosciutto and tightly wrap it around each of the bundles of asparagus. Place each bundle onto the lined trays. Drizzle a little olive oil over the top of the bundles, season with salt and pepper and sprinkle over the lemon zest. Bake in the oven for 12–15 minutes until the asparagus is cooked through and the prosciutto is turning a little bit crispy.

NOTES

- *You can swap the prosciutto for bacon if you prefer.*
- *If you want these a little spicier, drizzle over some chilli oil.*

STUFFED PEPPERS

Stuffed peppers are the sort of thing that I like as a main meal with a side salad, or as a side to something else, or because I just fancy doing something different with the veggies that I have left in the fridge. It's a great recipe for using up bits and bobs, and the little bit of melted and golden cheese topping and dab of spice brings the peppers up a notch.

MAKES: 8

PREP: 30 minutes
BAKE: 25–30 minutes
LASTS: 3+ days, at room temperature

4 large peppers
1 red pepper, finely chopped
½ red onion, finely chopped
Drizzle of olive oil
100g cooked rice
75g cherry tomatoes, quartered
75g chestnut mushrooms, finely chopped
½ courgette, finely chopped
4 garlic cloves, crushed
Salt and pepper
1 tsp chilli powder
1 tsp ground cumin
100g Cheddar cheese, grated

Preheat the oven to 200°C/180°C fan and line two large baking trays with parchment paper.

Cut each pepper in half from top to bottom, keeping the stalk attached. Scoop out the middle and place each half onto the trays. Bake in the oven for 15 minutes.

While the peppers are baking, make the filling. Add the chopped red pepper and red onion to a frying pan over a high heat with a drizzle of olive oil and cook for a few minutes. Then add the rice, tomatoes, mushrooms and courgette and fry for a couple of minutes to soften the vegetables. Add the garlic, salt, pepper, chilli powder, ground cumin and cooked rice and stir for a few minutes.

Remove the peppers from the oven and divide the filling between them. Pack the filling inside and then place back onto the trays. Sprinkle with the Cheddar, then bake for a further 10–15 minutes until the cheese is golden and melted.

NOTES

- Stuff your peppers with whatever you want – you just need about the same weights. Feel free to swap up the veggies you use, or even add some cooked crispy bacon lardons.

- You can use a packet of microwave rice or cook 35g (dried) rice from scratch.

YORKSHIRE PUDDINGS

We all know and love Yorkshire puddings, right? They're the ultimate addition to a roast dinner, but I could eat them every day to be honest. You only need a few ingredients, and you have something spectacular. These beautiful blog favourites are amazing served with Ultimate Roast Potatoes on page 194, or even with my Cheese and Broccoli Bake on page 154.

MAKES: 12

PREP: 20 minutes
BAKE: 15 minutes
LASTS: Best served
fresh

Vegetable oil
100g plain flour
2 eggs
100ml whole milk

Preheat the oven to 220°C/200°C fan and grab a 12-hole muffin tray. Pour a little vegetable oil into each hole of the muffin tray so it covers the bottom. Place into the oven while the oven preheats.

Add the flour and eggs to a jug and beat together. Add the milk and beat again until smooth. Carefully remove the muffin tray from the oven and divide the mixture between the 12 holes. Return to the oven for 15 minutes until the Yorkshire puddings have grown spectacularly and cooked through. Remove from the oven and enjoy.

NOTES

- *These are muffin-sized, but you can use a larger Yorkshire pudding dish and make 4–6 larger ones instead. These will require about 20 minutes cooking time.*

- *You can make the Yorkshires, then cool and freeze them for the future – just reheat in the oven when needed.*

ULTIMATE ROAST POTATOES

This is how my granny used to make roast potatoes, so I now make them every time and always get the best compliments – no wonder they're a blog favourite! The flavours of the garlic, thyme and rosemary bring the roast potatoes to a whole new level, and you will be amazed by how crispy they are. I find so many people don't roast their potatoes for long enough, so if you want to give them even longer to be even crispier, GO FOR IT!

SERVES: 4+

PREP: 20 minutes
BAKE: 40–45 minutes
LASTS: Best served fresh

1kg potatoes (I use Maris Piper), peeled and cut into 5–7.5cm pieces
150g goose fat
15g fresh thyme, chopped
15g fresh rosemary, chopped
Salt and pepper
50g plain flour
1 bulb of garlic

Boil the potatoes in a large pan of boiling salted water (that just about covers them) for about 5 minutes. Drain the water from the pan, put the lid on and vigorously shake the potatoes in the pan to create texture on the outside. Steam dry the potatoes while you preheat the oven to 220°C/200°C fan and get a large roasting tray.

Add the goose fat to the tray and heat in the oven while it preheats. Once hot, add the fresh thyme, fresh rosemary, salt and pepper to the pan of potatoes and mix. Add the flour and mix again. Tip the potatoes into the tray (carefully as the fat will be super-hot). Cut the garlic bulb in half and place into the tray to create flavour. Roast the potatoes in the oven for 15 minutes, then remove from the oven and turn the potatoes over. Repeat this process twice more until the potatoes have been roasting for 40–45 minutes in total.

NOTES

- I like my potatoes super crispy on the outside and fluffy on the inside, so they are roasted for quite a while. If your potatoes are browning too quickly, reduce the oven temperature by 20°C.

LOADED POTATO SKINS

Whether you want something delicious to have as a snack, as part of a BBQ, on the side of your main meal, or a dish that is just absolutely epic, this is the recipe. These potato skins are stuffed with potato, cheese, bacon and more to create a smooth but utterly delightful filling that you will just want to devour with a spoon before it even makes it to the potato skins.

MAKES: 8

PREP: 20 minutes
BAKE: 1 hour 50 minutes
COOL: 30 minutes
LASTS: 3+ days, in the fridge (but best served fresh)

4 large baking potatoes
1 tbsp olive oil
200g bacon lardons, cooked
3–4 spring onions, chopped, plus 2 finely chopped, to serve
100g full-fat soft cheese
150g Cheddar cheese, grated
1 egg
Salt and pepper

Preheat the oven to 220°C/200°C fan and get a large baking tray.

Pierce each potato a few times with a knife to prevent any explosions and rub the oil over them. Place onto a tray and bake in the oven for 30 minutes, then reduce the temperature to 200°C/180°C fan and bake for a further hour. Once baked, remove and leave to cool slightly.

Once cool enough to handle, cut the potatoes in half lengthways. Scoop out the middles of the potatoes and put the potato flesh into a large bowl. Add the cooked bacon lardons, spring onions, soft cheese, 100g of the Cheddar, egg and salt and pepper to the bowl. Mix together until you have a thick potato paste. Fill the potato halves with the filling, dividing equally between the potatoes. Place the potato halves into a large baking dish, and then sprinkle over the remaining Cheddar.

Bake in the oven for 20 minutes until the cheese is melted and turning golden. Remove from the oven and sprinkle over the finely chopped spring onions to serve.

NOTES

- *If you want vegetarian Loaded Potato Skins, use some roasted veg in place of the bacon or try a vegan bacon alternative.*

- *If you're short on time, you can bake the potatoes in the microwave to speed up the process, but the skins need to be cooked in the oven.*

- *These are great served with guacamole (see my recipe on page 160), or a little soured cream.*

MARMITE CHEESE ROLLS

Deliciously easy Marmite Cheese Rolls, with a Marmite and mozzarella centre and a simple homemade bread dough. Oh yes, heavenly. These blog beauties are an easy bake to share amongst your friends and family. Marmite and cheese is an endlessly wonderful pairing and combine it with the shape of a savoury cinnamon roll and you have a winner.

MAKES: 12

PREP: 30 minutes
PROVE: 2–3 hours
BAKE: 20–25 minutes
COOL: 30 minutes
LASTS: 3+ days, at room temperature (but best served fresh)

600g strong white bread flour, plus extra for dusting
14g dried active yeast
1 tbsp caster sugar
½ tsp sea salt
90g chilled unsalted butter, cubed
275ml whole milk
1 egg
Olive oil, for greasing
50g mozzarella, grated, for topping

Filling

100g Marmite
35g Parmesan, grated
150g mozzarella, grated

Add the flour, yeast, sugar and salt to a large bowl. Add the butter and rub in with your fingertips until it resembles breadcrumbs. Gently heat the milk in a pan or in the microwave until warm but not piping hot. Add the milk and egg to the dry ingredients. Knead the dough together for 7–10 minutes. It will be sticky at first, but it will soon come together. It should be springy to the touch, and not sticky. Transfer it into a lightly oiled bowl and cover with clingfilm. Leave it to rise for 1–2 hours, or until doubled in size.

Filling

Transfer the dough to a lightly floured work surface and roll it out into a large rectangle – mine was about 50 x 30cm. Carefully melt the Marmite in a heatproof bowl in short bursts in the microwave to make it easier to spread onto the dough.

Spread the Marmite all over the dough, up to the edges. Sprinkle over both cheeses. Roll the dough from long side to long side, to form a long sausage. Cut this evenly into 12 pieces and put them into a large rectangular baking dish (mine was 30 x 24cm). You want four rows of three, but they won't touch yet. Cover the dish with clingfilm and leave to rise for another hour or so until all the pieces touch.

Towards the end of the proving time, preheat the oven to 180°C/160°C fan so that when the dough has finished rising, you can put it straight in the oven. Sprinkle the mozzarella for the topping over the dough. Bake in the oven for 20–25 minutes until golden brown and cooked through. Leave to cool for about 30 minutes and then enjoy!

NOTES

- You can do the second prove in the fridge overnight. Shape the dough into the rolls and place into the baking dish, cover and place in the fridge. Let the dough come to room temperature the next day and bake.

- If you want to use fresh yeast, you will need double the amount. Some dried yeasts need activating, so read the packet instructions and add to the warmed milk if yours does.

SUN-DRIED TOMATO BREAD

If you want a change from your normal white loaf, then try this insanely delicious Sun-Dried Tomato Bread. It makes everything so much better and will elevate your toastie game so much. I LOVE making bread at home as it's the perfect activity to take your time over on a rainy day and having fun with the flavours makes it even better. Serve this bread on the side of a soup or use in a sandwich for something out-of-this-world tasty.

SERVES: 8–10

PREP: 15 minutes
PROVE: 1–2 hours
BAKE: 35–40 minutes
LASTS: 2+ days, at room temperature (but best served fresh)

550g strong white bread flour, plus extra for dusting

7g dried active yeast

25g caster sugar

1 tsp sea salt

100g chilled unsalted butter, cubed

175ml warm water

1 egg

3 tbsp sun-dried tomato paste

30ml oil (from tomato jar)

75g sun-dried tomatoes, halved

1 tsp dried rosemary

Oil, for greasing

Add the flour, yeast, sugar and salt to a large bowl. Add the butter and rub in with your fingertips until the mixture resembles breadcrumbs. Add the warm water, egg, sun-dried tomato paste and oil and knead together for 7–10 minutes. It will be sticky at first, but it will soon come together. It should be springy to the touch, and not sticky. Towards the end, add the sun-dried tomatoes and dried rosemary and knead in. Transfer to a lightly oiled bowl and cover with clingfilm. Leave it to rise for 1–2 hours, or until doubled in size.

Once the dough has risen, remove it from the bowl and knock back slightly to deflate some of the air. Shape the dough into a round, and place onto a lightly floured baking tray.

Preheat the oven to 220°C/200°C fan.

Bake in the oven for 15 minutes, then reduce the temperature to 200°C/180°C fan and bake for a further 20–25 minutes. Check that the bread is ready by tapping the bottom – it should make a hollow sound.

NOTES

- If you want to add another flavour, add 100g chopped olives.

- You can leave out the chunks of sun-dried tomato if you prefer and just use the paste.

CAMEMBERT TEAR AND SHARE BREAD

We've all been there, right? When you want something so badly, but it seems like such an effort? Well, I am here to help and ensure all your Camembert cheese dreams come true. This dough is so easy to make, and you will want to make it over and over again; whether that's for yourself, a girls' night, dinner, or even a special occasion. The garlic and herb-flavoured bread, surrounding a gooey and freshly baked camembert is almost *too much* but in reality, it's just heaven in every single bite.

SERVES: 4+

PREP: 2 hours
PROVE: 1–2½ hours
BAKE: 25 minutes
COOL: 10 minutes
LASTS: Best served fresh

450g strong white bread flour
7g dried active yeast
25g caster sugar
1 tsp sea salt
1 tsp mixed herbs
1 tsp garlic powder
1 tsp onion powder
100g chilled unsalted butter, cubed
200ml whole milk
1 egg
Olive oil, for greasing
3 garlic cloves, finely chopped
1 Camembert
Drizzle of honey

Topping

50g unsalted butter
10g chopped fresh parsley

Add the flour, yeast, sugar, salt, mixed herbs, garlic and onion powders to a large bowl. Add the butter and rub it in with your fingertips until the mixture resembles breadcrumbs.

Gently heat the milk in a pan or in the microwave until warm but not piping hot. Add the milk and egg to the dry ingredients. Knead the dough together for 7–10 minutes. It will be sticky at first, but it will soon come together. It should be springy to touch, and not sticky. Transfer to a lightly oiled bowl and cover with clingfilm. Leave it to rise for 1–2 hours, or until doubled in size.

Once the dough has doubled in size, grab a large round baking dish.

Insert pieces of garlic into the Camembert, then drizzle over some honey. Place the cheese in the middle of the dish. Take the risen dough and shape it into a ball. Chop this into 16 pieces – I cut the ball in half, half again etc until I have 16 pieces. Roll each piece into a ball and then place around the Camembert, with gaps between each piece. Cover the dish with an oiled piece of clingfilm and leave the dough to rise again for about 20–30 minutes. While it proves, preheat the oven to 200°C/180°C fan.

Once all the dough balls are touching each other, bake in the oven for 25 minutes.

Topping

While the bread bakes, melt the butter and mix in the parsley. Remove the bread from the oven brush over the parsley butter.

NOTES

- *The bread also works well as plain dough balls – bake them without the Camembert and dip into butter instead.*

BAGELS

Whenever I have a bagel, I just can't get enough. Sweet or savoury, they are delicious. I absolutely love filling mine to the brim with anything from the classic soft cheese and smoked salmon combo to a ton of chocolate spread, to egg and bacon. Bagels are such a versatile all-rounder, and you can freeze these and toast them from frozen to enjoy at a moment's notice.

MAKES: 8

PREP: 20 minutes
PROVE: 1+ hours
BAKE: 27–30 minutes
COOL: 30 minutes
LASTS: Lasts: 3+ days, at room temperature

350ml warm water
10g fast action dried yeast
1 tsp sea salt, plus extra for sprinkling
65g caster sugar
575g strong white bread flour, plus extra for dusting
Oil, for greasing

Add the warm water and yeast to a large bowl, whisk together and leave to sit for a minute or two. Add the salt and 15g of the sugar and whisk to combine. Add the flour and mix with a spatula to combine. Knead the dough for a few minutes if it's a little sticky. Place the dough onto a lightly floured work surface and knead for 5 minutes until you have a smooth round ball of dough. Place the dough into a lightly oiled bowl and leave to rest for an hour or so.

Towards the end of the proving time, preheat the oven to 220°C/200°C fan and line two baking trays with parchment paper.

In a large pan, pour 2 litres of water and the remaining 50g sugar and bring to the boil. Remove 100g pieces of dough from the dough and, on a very lightly floured work surface, roll into sausages about 20cm long. Form each sausage into a circle and seal the ends together well.

Once the water is boiling, drop in the bagels 1–2 at a time, so you don't overcrowd the pan, and boil for 2 minutes. Remove from the water and drain off as much water as possible with a slotted spoon, then place onto the lined baking trays.

Sprinkle each bagel with chunky sea salt. Bake in the oven for 27–30 minutes until golden brown and delicious. Leave to cool for 30 minutes, then enjoy.

NOTES

- *You can flavour the bagels in various ways. Sprinkle on sesame seeds, add 1–2 teaspoons of ground cinnamon to the dough or even add some mixed herbs and garlic.*

BACON TURNOVERS

Is anyone else ever drawn to the smell of freshly baked pastry and freshly cooked bacon? Because I just can't help myself. I could have just eaten a full meal, and I will catch a sniff of those smells and be hungry immediately. Luckily these savoury turnovers are so easy to bake, as well as a real crowd-pleaser, so are perfect for sharing. They have a slightly cheesy filling with a hint of mustard, topped with crispy bacon – perfect for any time of day.

MAKES: 6

PREP: 10 minutes
BAKE: 20 minutes
LASTS: 3+ days, in the fridge (but best served fresh)

1 x 350g sheet of puff pastry

Plain flour, for dusting

1 tsp English or wholegrain mustard

75g soft cheese

Salt and pepper

6 rashers of bacon

125g mature Cheddar cheese, grated

1 egg, beaten

Preheat the oven to 220°C/200°C fan and line two large baking trays with parchment paper.

Put the sheet of puff pastry onto a lightly floured work surface and cut into six squares. Spread a little mustard onto the middle of each square. Dollop the soft cheese in the middle of the squares and spread slightly. Sprinkle with salt and pepper. Add a slice of bacon on top – I do this diagonally. Sprinkle over the Cheddar. Fold two opposite corners into the middle of each pastry square and seal by pressing together and brushing on a little beaten egg. Brush beaten egg over the outside of the pastries and transfer to the trays.

Bake in the oven for 20 minutes, or until golden.

NOTES

- *If you don't want to cook your own bacon or you want something even easier, you can use slices of cooked ham, or any other cooked meat.*
- *These can be prepped and frozen on trays, then transferred to a container and baked as and when you want them. Simply add 2 minutes to the baking time.*

CHEESE SCONES

I am a true fan of all things scones (as are my blog readers) but savoury scones are in a completely different ballpark. I love a freshly baked cheese scone that is still warm and topped with a slab of butter and maybe a little Marmite, but that's only one of the options. Extra cheese, a bit of ham, dunked in soup – the choices are endless. These deliciously versatile Cheese Scones have a little spice to them with some mustard powder and cayenne pepper – perfect for all the family to enjoy, and you can even get little ones involved in the making too.

MAKES: 8

PREP: 30 minutes
BAKE: 12–15 minutes
COOL: 30 minutes
LASTS: 3+ days, at room temperature (but best served fresh)

300g self-raising flour, plus extra for dusting

60g chilled unsalted butter, cubed

½ tsp mustard powder

½ tsp cayenne pepper

¼ tsp salt and pepper

100g mature Cheddar cheese, grated

25g Parmesan, grated

150ml whole milk, plus extra for brushing

Preheat the oven to 220°C/200°C fan and line a large baking tray with parchment paper. Place the tray in the oven to preheat.

Add the flour, butter, mustard powder, cayenne pepper, salt and pepper to a large mixing bowl and mix together with your fingertips until the mixture resembles breadcrumbs. Add the Cheddar, Parmesan and milk. Mix the mixture together with a spatula until a dough is formed.

Tip the dough out onto a lightly floured work surface and gently pat the dough down to about 4cm thick. Use a 4–5cm cutter to cut out scones and place onto the preheated baking tray. Brush the tops of the scones with extra milk, and sprinkle with extra cheese if desired. Bake in the oven for 12–15 minutes, or until golden. Leave to cool slightly and then enjoy warm or cool fully and enjoy cold.

NOTES

- You can switch up the cheese that you use for these scones by using a milder cheese or leaving out the Parmesan – just remember any 'dry' or 'hard' cheese works well.
- You can reheat the scones in the oven at 170°C/150°C fan for 5 minutes.

Sweet Treats

VANILLA SPRINKLE DOUGHNUTS

Over the years I am sure we have all devoured a sprinkle-covered doughnut. They are an absolute classic and something I'd like to eat all day, every day if I could. But it's an effort (and expensive) to go out and buy doughnuts all the time. So being able to bake some super easy doughnuts at home, and then have some fun decorating them is SO much better! The fact that they are baked makes these fan favourite doughnuts so much easier to make because you don't need a tonne of oil.

MAKES: 15

PREP: 30 minutes
BAKE: 10–13 minutes
COOL: 1 hour
DECORATE: 20 minutes
LASTS: 3+ days, at room temperature

150g unsalted butter
150g caster sugar
1 egg
175g plain flour
1 tsp baking powder
Pinch of salt
100ml whole milk
1 tsp vanilla extract
Olive oil, for greasing

Decoration
300g icing sugar
1–3 tbsp water
1 tsp pink food colouring
100g rainbow sprinkles

Preheat the oven to 180°C/160°C fan.

In a large bowl, beat the butter and sugar and together until creamy. Add the egg and beat again. Add the flour, baking powder and salt and beat, then add the milk and vanilla extract and mix until smooth. Grease a doughnut mould and then pipe or spoon the doughnut mixture into the moulds. The mixture should be slightly below the edge of the mould.

Bake in the oven for 10–13 minutes, or until the doughnuts are starting to come away from the edges of the moulds. Leave to cool for a few minutes before turning out onto a wire rack to cool completely.

Decoration
Add the icing sugar to a bowl, then gradually add the water and mix until you have a thick icing. Colour the icing bright pink with the food colouring. Dunk the top of each doughnut into the pink icing and place onto a lined tray – sprinkle with rainbow sprinkles as you go. Leave the icing to set.

BRONUTS

Say hello to your new top bake... Bronuts. If you haven't got what they are from the title, or the photos, these blog favourites are triple chocolate brownie doughnuts, and they are utterly delicious. Bronuts have become the new craze, and while they may sound a little weird, they are delightfully moreish. They are also incredibly easy to make, so you should definitely give them a go and impress family and friends with something a bit different.

MAKES: 15

PREP: 30 minutes
BAKE: 16–18 minutes
COOL: 1 hour
DECORATE: 30 minutes
LASTS: 3+ days, at
room temperature

200g dark chocolate
200g unsalted butter
4 eggs
275g soft light brown sugar
100g plain flour
50g cocoa powder
200g milk chocolate chips

Decoration

125g white chocolate
125g milk chocolate
Chocolates
Sprinkles

Preheat the oven to 180°C/160°C fan and grease 2–3 doughnut moulds.

In a heatproof bowl, break up the dark chocolate into pieces and add the butter. Microwave in short bursts or set the bowl over a pan of simmering water (bain-marie) until smooth. Leave to cool for 10 minutes.

In a separate bowl, whisk the eggs and sugar together until the mixture is mousse-like and has doubled in size. Pour in the melted chocolate mixture and fold together. Add the flour and cocoa powder and fold through. Finally, fold through the chocolate chips. Carefully pour or pipe the bronut mixture into the moulds. Bake in the oven for 16–18 minutes, then leave to cool fully in the moulds.

Decoration

Add each chocolate to separate heatproof bowls big enough to dunk the bronuts into, then microwave in short bursts or set the bowls over a pan of simmering water (bain-marie) until smooth. Dunk half of the bronuts into the white chocolate, and half into the milk chocolate. Drizzle the leftover milk chocolate onto the white chocolate-dipped bronuts, and the white chocolate onto the milk chocolate ones. Add a chocolate, sprinkles or anything else you fancy and leave the chocolate to set.

NOTES

- The dark chocolate is very important to the flavour here, so please don't switch that, but the milk chocolate chips can be swapped for white or dark ones.

- As these don't rise much, I tend to fill the moulds to just before the mould line.

BAKEWELL SCONES

These beautiful little parcels of heaven are so delightful and moreish. I love to serve mine with some clotted cream and a cherry conserve, but you can serve them however you like. These are a perfect make ahead option as you can prep the scone dough, shape and then freeze – you just need to add 2 minutes to the baking time.

MAKES: 8

PREP: 30 minutes
BAKE: 10–13 minutes
COOL: 30 minutes
LASTS: 3+ days, at
room temperature

100g chilled unsalted butter,
   cubed
325g self-raising flour, plus extra
   for dusting
150g ground almonds
50g caster sugar
1 tsp baking powder
½ tsp sea salt
190ml whole milk
1 tsp lemon juice
1 tsp almond extract
150g glacé cherries, chopped
1 egg, beaten
30g flaked almonds

Preheat the oven to 220°C/200°C fan and line a large baking tray with parchment paper.

Place the tray in the oven to preheat.

Add the butter, flour, ground almonds, sugar, baking powder and salt to a large bowl. Rub the ingredients together with your fingertips until the mixture resembles breadcrumbs. Warm the milk in a pan on the hob or in the microwave, then pour into the mixture with the lemon juice and almond extract. Mix the dough together with a spatula, adding the glacé cherries.

On a floured work surface, tip out the scone dough and flatten with your hands until 5cm thick. Cut out eight scones using a 6–7cm cutter. Carefully place onto the preheated tray, then glaze with the beaten egg. Sprinkle over the flaked almonds, then bake in the oven for 10–13 minutes, or until golden. Leave to cool slightly and then enjoy.

NOTES

- *You can use fresh cherries, or other fruit, instead of the glacé cherries if you prefer– just reduce the amount by 50g.*

STUFFED MUG CAKE

While we all love something sweet and delicious such as a cookie, or a slice of cake or cheesecake, sometimes you just want a super-quick treat that you can eat in minutes, and this Stuffed Mug Cake is the answer. The sponge is made from four simple storecupboard ingredients, then stuffed with whatever you fancy – I've given some of my favourites below. The perfect bake for when you want something warm, gooey and tasty in just 5 minutes.

MAKES: 1

PREP: 2 minutes
BAKE: 1–1½ minutes
LASTS: Best served
fresh

Add the flour, sugar, oil and milk to a mug. Mix together until smooth. Spoon in your chosen stuffing. Microwave on high for 1–1½ minutes until cooked. The cooking time may vary as all microwaves are different – you are looking for a solid top to the cake, but gooeyness in the middle. Enjoy!

NOTES

- *You can make the mug cake chocolate-flavoured by replacing 15g of the self-raising flour with 15g cocoa powder.*

60g self-raising flour
30g caster sugar
1 tbsp sunflower oil
4 tbsp whole milk or vegan milk

Stuffing

Choose one of the following:
1 tbsp speculoos spread (I use Biscoff)
1 tbsp chocolate spread
1 tbsp crunchy or smooth peanut butter
25g chunk of chocolate of your choice

ICED BUNS

When I was a child, I would always beg my mum or dad for a packet of iced buns when we were at the supermarket, or I'd ask for one at a bakery. I don't know what it was, but I was simply obsessed. I now love being able to make my own version of these retro classics at home, flavouring my wonderfully light dough with a hint of vanilla. I'll have three with my cup of tea, please.

MAKES: 12

PREP: 30 minutes
PROVE: 2–3 hours
BAKE: 20–22 minutes
COOL: 1 hour
DECORATE: 15 minutes
LASTS: 3+ days, at room temperature (but best served fresh)

300g strong white bread flour
300g plain flour, plus extra for dusting
14g dried yeast
75g caster sugar
90g chilled unsalted butter, cubed
275ml whole milk
1 tsp vanilla extract
1 egg
Olive oil, for greasing

Decoration

500–600g icing sugar
1 tsp vanilla extract
4–5 tbsp water
Pink food colouring (optional)

Add both flours, the dried yeast, sugar and butter to a large bowl. Rub the mixture together with your fingertips until it resembles breadcrumbs. Heat the milk in a pan or in the microwave until warm, then pour into the mixture, along with the vanilla extract and egg. Knead together for 7–10 minutes until the dough is smooth and elastic. Transfer the dough to a lightly oiled bowl and cover with clingfilm. Leave to rise for 1–2 hours, or until doubled in size.

Transfer the dough to a lightly floured work surface and shape into a disc. Cut the dough into 12 portions – I did this by cutting the circle with a sharp knife into half, then half again, etc until I had 12 pieces. Shape each section into a rectangle and line up in two rows of six onto a large, lined baking tray, with space in between each one. Cover the buns with clingfilm and leave to rise again for 30–60 minutes until they have risen and are just about touching. Towards the end of the proving time, preheat the oven to 180°C/160°C fan.

Remove the clingfilm and bake in the oven for 20–22 minutes, or until golden brown. Leave to cool.

Decoration

Add the icing sugar to a large bowl with the vanilla extract. Gradually add the water until you have a thick paste. Add a drop of pink food colouring if you fancy pink icing. Drizzle and smother the icing over the buns. Leave to set for 30–60 minutes, then devour.

NOTES

- You can use all strong white bread flour if you want a slightly denser texture, or you can use all plain flour if you want a slightly more cake-like texture.

- The dried yeast may need activating depending on which brand you use – check the packet instructions. If it does, add it to the warm milk before using.

- You can top the iced buns with coloured icing, or even make it chocolate-flavoured by swapping 40g icing sugar for 40g cocoa powder.

PEANUT BUTTER TRUFFLES

These truffles are so easy to make and ever so slightly addictive. You may wonder where the chocolate and cream are, but using peanut butter, biscuits, sugar and soft cheese gives a delightfully different texture to these truffles. I decorate mine with milk chocolate first, then drizzle over some melted peanut butter and finely chopped peanuts to finish them off. These would make the perfect edible gift for the peanut butter lover in your life.

MAKES: 20

PREP: 30 minutes
SET: 2 hours
DECORATE: 15 minutes
LASTS: 5+ days,
in the fridge

100g digestive biscuits
200g smooth or crunchy peanut butter
200g full-fat soft cheese
75g icing sugar

Decoration

300g milk chocolate
35g smooth peanut butter
25g peanuts, finely chopped

Finely crush the biscuits in a food processor or in a bowl with a rolling pin. Add the peanut butter, soft cheese and icing sugar and mix together to make a thick paste. Using two teaspoons, scoop truffle-sized portions, then roll into balls and place onto a lined baking tray. Freeze the truffles for 1 hour until solid.

Decoration

Add the chocolate to a heatproof bowl and microwave in short bursts or set the bowl over a pan of simmering water (bain-marie) until smooth. Dip each truffle into the melted chocolate and place back onto the lined tray. Melt the peanut butter in a heatproof bowl in the microwave or in a pan on a low heat until smooth, then drizzle onto the truffles, and sprinkle over the peanuts. Leave to set in the fridge for 1 hour and then enjoy.

NOTES

- You can use other biscuits in place of the digestive biscuits such as cookies, gingernuts, cookies and cream biscuits etc.
- You can use smooth or crunchy peanut butter in the filling.

LEMON TRUFFLES

The dreamy combination of lemon and white chocolate brings sharpness, sourness and sweetness. Add it to a truffle and you have one of my favourite sweet treats EVER! These are silky smooth, covered in a layer of white chocolate for a slight crunch and oh my days... tasty. I decided to decorate mine with white chocolate mixed with a yellow drizzle to jazz them up slightly, but you can customise them however you fancy, or theme them for a gift or a party.

MAKES: 20

PREP: 30 minutes
SET: 2 hours
DECORATE: 15 minutes
LASTS: 5+ days,
in the fridge

500g white chocolate
15g unsalted butter
100ml double cream
1 tsp lemon extract

Decoration

300g white chocolate
½ tsp oil-based yellow food
colouring

Add the white chocolate to a heatproof bowl along with the butter, double cream and lemon extract. Melt in the microwave in short bursts, stirring well each time, until the mixture is smooth. Using two teaspoons, scoop truffle-sized portions, then roll into balls and place onto a lined baking tray. Freeze the truffles for 1 hour until solid.

Decoration

Melt the white chocolate in a heatproof bowl. Separate 50g of the melted chocolate into a new bowl, add the yellow food colouring and combine. Dip each truffle into the melted white chocolate and place back onto the lined tray. Drizzle with the yellow chocolate. Leave to set in the fridge for 1 hour and then enjoy.

NOTES

- You can decorate the truffles with other types of chocolate if you prefer – dark chocolate is delicious as a contrast to the white chocolate lemon centre.

- Other flavourings can be used if you just want to use the recipe as a base – try almond, coffee or peppermint extract.

COCONUT ICE

Coconut Ice is a retro classic treat and enjoyed by so many people. You only need four ingredients, and it's so incredibly easy that you will want to make it every single day. You don't have to use the food colouring if you don't fancy it (or don't have it), but it's a part of the classic Coconut Ice look. I love making this when I want something simple, sweet and tasty but it makes a great gift, or it's the perfect treat to make with your kids when they need something to do!

MAKES: 25

PREP: 30 minutes
SET: 3–4+ hours
LASTS: 7+ days at
room temperature

300g condensed milk
400g icing sugar
250g desiccated coconut
½ tsp red food colouring

Line a 20cm square tin with parchment paper.

In a large bowl, mix the condensed milk, icing sugar and desiccated coconut with a spatula until combined into a thick paste. Pour half into another bowl and add the red food colouring. Mix until it's evenly distributed, and the mixture has turned pink. Pour one of the colours into the lined tin and spread. Pour the other colour on top and spread again.

Set in the fridge for 3–4 hours, or overnight, until solid. Once set, cut into small squares with a sharp knife and enjoy.

NOTES

- *You can elevate this Coconut Ice by covering the pieces in melted chocolate once they have set and been portioned. I love using dark chocolate for this.*

COOKIE DOUGH PRETZEL BITES

As we all know by now, I love cookie dough. Whether it stays 'raw' like in this recipe, or is baked into cookies, cookie bars, giant cookies and so on... So when you add cookie dough to delicious crunchy salted pretzels, then dip them both into chocolate? Oh my... HELLO. These easy bites are perfect for when you want to whip up a sweet treat at a moment's notice – heaven in every mouthful.

MAKES: 20–25

PREP: 30 minutes
BAKE: 5 minutes
DECORATE: 30 minutes
SET: 45–60 minutes
LASTS: 3+ days, at room temperature

200g plain flour
125g unsalted butter, at room temperature
165g soft light brown sugar
1 tsp vanilla extract
35ml whole or vegan milk
175g milk or dark chocolate, finely chopped
40–50 salted pretzels
200g milk chocolate, melted

Preheat oven to 200°C/180°C fan and line a large baking tray with parchment paper. Sprinkle over the flour evenly and bake in the oven for 5 minutes. Transfer to a bowl and leave to cool for 5 minutes.

In a separate bowl, beat the butter and sugar together until combined. Add the baked flour, vanilla extract, milk and chocolate and beat to form a cookie dough. Divide the cookie dough into 20–25 pieces using spoons.

Roll the cookie dough pieces into balls, then carefully sandwich each one between two pretzels. Place them onto a lined tray. Dip half of each pretzel cookie dough bite into the melted chocolate, and then place back onto the lined tray. Chill the bites for 45–60 minutes until the chocolate has set.

NOTES

- You can make the cookie dough chocolate-flavoured by swapping 25g of the plain flour for 25g cocoa powder.

- You can use caster sugar instead of the soft light brown soft sugar, but the brown sugar brings a wonderful caramel flavour to the cookie dough.

- The chocolate can be any flavour you fancy for the coating, and the cookie dough.

HONEYCOMB FUDGE

Fudge is so easy to make when it uses condensed milk like this fan favourite. Just three simple ingredients and you have a delightful sweet treat. I decided to use milk chocolate for this fudge as it complements the honeycomb, but you can use any other sweet instead if you fancy. If you want to try making your own honeycomb, you can find my recipe in my first book, *Jane's Patisserie*.

MAKES: 30 pieces

PREP: 15 minutes
BAKE: 10 minutes
SET: 2–3 hours
LASTS: 7+ days,
in the fridge

397g tin condensed milk
500g milk chocolate
300g chocolate-covered
honeycomb, chopped (I use
Crunchie)

Line a 23cm square tin with parchment paper and set aside.

Melt the condensed milk and chocolate in a medium pan over a very low heat until the mixture is smooth. Alternatively, you can melt the mixture in the microwave in 20-second bursts, stirring well each time.

Once melted, take the fudge off the heat. Stir through most of the chopped honeycomb, then the pour into the tin and spread. Top with the remaining chopped honeycomb. Set in the fridge for 2–3 hours, or until solid. Cut into 2.5–5cm pieces with a sharp knife and enjoy.

NOTES

- *If you want to use dark chocolate, you need to use 400g.*
- *If you want to use white chocolate, you need to use 600g.*
- *You can use any shop-bought honeycomb chocolate bar, or even a homemade one!*

CHERRY BAKEWELL FUDGE

Cherry and almond is a match made in heaven, and I will shove it into any recipe I can – this time, it's fudge. Marrying a simple white chocolate and condensed milk fudge with glacé cherries, almonds and a little crunch of biscuit is so quick that you'd be silly to not give it a try! Whip up a batch to share with family and friends.

MAKES: 30 pieces

PREP: 15 minutes
BAKE: 15 minutes
SET: 3–4+ hours
LASTS: 5+ days, at room temperature or in the fridge

395g condensed milk
600g white chocolate
1–2 tsp almond extract
200g glacé cherries
100g digestive biscuits, chopped (optional)
15g flaked almonds, toasted (optional)

Line a 23cm square tin with parchment paper and set aside.

Add the condensed milk and chocolate to a bowl and heat in short bursts in the microwave, stirring well each time, until smooth. Alternatively, add the two ingredients to a large pan and melt over a low heat, stirring constantly, until smooth. Add the almond extract, glacé cherries and chopped biscuits and stir through.

Pour into the lined tin and smooth over. Sprinkle on toasted almond flakes if you want.

Set in the fridge for 3–4 hours, or overnight. Cut into squares with a sharp knife and enjoy!

NOTES

- The addition of biscuits is completely optional – feel free to leave them out.

- If you don't have flaked almonds, don't worry – just leave them out.

- You can swap the white chocolate for 500g milk chocolate or 400g dark chocolate.

MINI MERINGUES

I think most people have enjoyed meringue at some point in their lives, so here are my simple ones to make at home. These little poops of goodness (because let's be honest now, they are meringue poops) are colourful, easy, and a great thing to make with kids, or as a part of a bigger dessert. I made mine super colourful, but you can bake a plain version, make them into an Eton Mess Rocky Road (see my recipe on page 72), or decorate them to enjoy as a fancier dessert for a celebration.

MAKES: 30+

PREP: 30 minutes
BAKE: 80–90 minutes
COOL: 1 hour
DECORATE: 10 minutes
SET: 30 minutes
LASTS: 7+ days, at room temperature

3 egg whites
150g caster sugar
1 tsp vanilla, lemon, orange or almond extract
1 tsp food colouring – red, orange, yellow, green, blue, purple, or several (optional)

Decoration (optional)
100g white, milk or dark chocolate

Preheat the oven to 110°C/90°C fan and line 2–3 large baking trays with parchment paper.

Add the egg whites into a bowl and whisk on a high speed until soft peaks form. Then start to add the sugar 1 teaspoon at a time, whisking continuously. Once all the sugar has been added, flavour the meringue to your preference. The meringue should be smooth and glossy once finished.

Prep a piping bag with a jumbo round piping tip. Using a small brush, brush food colouring up the inside of the piping bag. I did a stripe of each colour to make a rainbow. Add the meringue to the piping bag. Pipe dollops of meringue onto the baking trays. Bake in the oven for 80–90 minutes, or until a meringue lifts off the paper easily. Leave the meringues to cool in the oven with the door shut.

Decoration

Add your chosen chocolate to a heatproof bowl and microwave in short bursts or set the bowl over a pan of simmering water (bain-marie) until smooth. Dip the base of the meringues into the chocolate and place back onto the paper. Leave to set fully.

NOTES

- For an extra level of decoration, dip the melted chocolate into sprinkles before placing back onto the paper.

- The chocolate is an optional extra, and so is the colouring.

S'MORES DIP

This simple two-ingredient sweet dip makes a delicious treat – ideal for dipping your favourite ingredients! Chocolate and marshmallows are a winning combination and one of my guilty pleasures, especially when they're both melted, so it's no wonder this recipe is a fan favourite. An easy indulgent dessert, perfect for putting in the centre of the table and letting everyone dip to their heart's content.

SERVES: 6–8

PREP: 10 minutes
BAKE: 10–20 seconds
LASTS: Best served fresh

200–400g milk chocolate
200–400g marshmallows

To Dip

Biscuits
Strawberries
Marshmallows
Chocolate
Apples

In a large heatproof dish, add the chocolate to the bottom. Place the marshmallows all over the top so that they cover the chocolate. Microwave the dish in 20-second bursts until the chocolate and marshmallows start to melt (but don't explode!).

Once they have started to melt, place the dish under a preheated grill for 10–20 seconds to toast the marshmallows and then remove from the heat. Leave to cool for a couple of minutes and then dip away!

NOTES

- *You can use any flavour chocolate you want – milk, dark, white, flavoured and so on!*

- *I use regular marshmallows, but mini marshmallows also work well – the melting time will be quicker though.*

PARTY RINGS

Party rings are a retro childhood classic, and I still adore them. I love the biscuit with the crunchy icing on top, and the colours are so pretty. However, if you make them at home, you can create whatever shapes you want, then decorate them in the colours of your choice. You can stick to a theme or just have fun experimenting with different colours. I used a mix of pink and yellow, but you do you! Perfect for a party or just when you want a taste of nostalgia.

MAKES: 12

PREP: 15 minutes
CHILL: 2 hours
BAKE: 10–13 minutes
COOL: 1 hour
DECORATE: 10 minutes
SET: 1–2 hours
LASTS: 3+ days, at room temperature

100g chilled unsalted butter, cubed
175g plain flour, plus extra for dusting
35g cornflour
65g caster sugar
1 egg, plus 1 egg yolk
2 tsp vanilla extract

Decoration

250g icing sugar
3–6 tbsp water or lemon juice
1 tsp pink food colouring
1 tsp yellow food colouring

Add the butter, flour, cornflour and sugar to a bowl and rub together with your fingertips until the mixture resembles breadcrumbs. Add the egg, egg yolk and vanilla extract and mix together until a dough is formed. Wrap the dough in clingfilm and chill for 1 hour. Meanwhile, line 3–4 large baking trays with baking parchment.

On a lightly floured surface, roll out the dough until 3mm thick. Cut out 12 discs using a 7cm cutter, then cut out a hole in the middle of each one with a 3cm cutter. Place the biscuits onto the lined trays as you go, re-rolling the dough until you have used it all up. Chill the biscuits for 1 hour and preheat the oven to 180°C/160°C fan.

Bake in the oven for 10–13 minutes or until golden and baked through. Leave to cool completely on the trays.

Decoration

Add 100g of icing sugar to one bowl, 100g to another bowl, and 50g to a final bowl. Add 1–2 tablespoons of water or lemon juice to each of the 100g bowls, and 1–2 teaspoons to the 50g bowl. Add pink food colouring to one of the 100g bowls and mix until combined. Add yellow food colouring to the other 100g bowl and mix until combined. Mix the 50g bowl together until combined. Dip half of the biscuits carefully into the pink icing and the other half into the yellow icing. Drizzle the white icing over all of the biscuits and then use a cocktail stick to drag lines in alternating directions to give a feathered look. Leave the biscuits to set on the lined trays for 1–2 hours, and then enjoy.

NOTES

- *You can flavour the icing if you want using strong flavours. One teaspoon of lemon, orange or vanilla extract work wonderfully!*

- *The biscuit dough can be used as a base for other decorations – it makes a great base for fondant icing.*

Free-From Every Day

So, I am not vegan or gluten free, but I know that plenty of my followers are and many of us may also need to cook or bake for someone who is, so this little section is designed to give inspiration and suggestions for useful swaps to satisfy any free-from needs.

A lot of foods are naturally vegan and/or gluten free so, first and foremost, it's all about reading the labels. Dairy, eggs and gluten can all sneak into food where you least expect it, so it's very important to check the labels on everything you buy to make sure you know exactly what it contains. Accidentally consuming something that you aren't used to digesting or are intolerant to can make you quite unwell, so this is a crucial first step.

These days, there are so many good substitutes for core ingredients, so baking vegan or gluten-free is so much more accessible – and I love that. You might find that the textures change a little when making the swaps, but don't worry they'll still taste just as delicious! Simple switches and tweaks mean that you can still create the most wonderful bakes that everyone can enjoy, without any compromise on flavour.

As well as my basic swaps and tips, I've included a few core recipes in this section so that you can make my most popular bakes vegan or gluten-free. Start with my core recipes and then branch out to experiment with different toppings and flavours as you fancy, just make sure that your flavours and toppings are free-from, too!

Vegan Baking Swaps

- **MILKS**
  Instead of dairy milk, I prefer to use almond, soy or other nut milks. It's a straight 1:1 swap.

- **CREAMS**
  There are some good dairy-free alternatives now, you just need to make sure they are full-fat. Or coconut cream works well.

- **BUTTERMILK**
  Add 15ml of lemon juice to 250ml vegan milk to make homemade vegan buttermilk.

- **BUTTER**
  Try to find a dairy-free alternative that is as firm as possible. Spreads should be avoided as the oil content is higher to make them softer.

- **EGGS**
  1 tablespoon of flax seeds or chia seeds mixed with 3 tablespoons of water makes a good alternative to replace an egg in some bakes. Other good swaps include 60g of apple sauce, half a mashed ripe banana, or 3 tablespoons of aquafaba (tinned chickpea water).

- **CHOCOLATE**
  There are many good dairy-free alternatives out there, but some brands of dark chocolate are naturally vegan, so do check the labels.

- **HONEY**
  Maple syrup works wonders as a replacement.

- **CHEESE**
  I have often made my savoury dishes vegan using straight swaps. Nutritional yeast is lovely to add to a cheesy dish as it brings the cheesy flavour, on top of using a vegan cheese alternative.

- **MEAT**
  You can find some brilliant vegan meat alternatives out there now such as fake chicken, sausages etc, and these all work well. Mushrooms are a brilliant swap to give you a 'meaty' texture, as well as pressed tofu.

Gluten-Free Baking Swaps

- ### FLOURS
  Most flours have gluten-free alternatives available now, and they work well. The texture can vary slightly, but xanthan gum is a useful addition.

- ### XANTHAN GUM
  It can vary, but a good start is about ¼ teaspoon of xanthan gum per 150g of flour. It creates a bind in the ingredients that better replicates bakes containing gluten resulting in a better texture.

- ### CORNFLOUR
  Some bakes, such as cupcakes, can have their texture improved by using cornflour. A lot of custard powders contain cornflour and are gluten free – custard powder can improve the texture of a bake tenfold.

- ### BISCUITS
  Again, gluten-free versions work perfectly. When making a biscuit base, add the butter slowly as some may need slightly less to make a good base.

- ### PASTA
  Rice and lentil pastas are often gluten free, but the gluten-free pasta options work perfectly.

VEGAN COOKIES

These cookies are easy, delicious, gooey, crunchy and heavenly in every bite. Cookies are one of the best things you can bake, and they are always a crowd-pleaser, so these Vegan Cookies will be a winner. A delicious basic chocolate chip cookie can take you far and can be used as a base to make all sort of flavours that you fancy!

MAKES: 12

PREP: 20 minutes
CHILL: 30 minutes+
BAKE: 10–11 minutes
COOL: 15 minutes
LASTS: 3–4+ days, at room temperature

125g vegan butter
175g soft light brown sugar
1 tsp vanilla extract
300g plain flour
1½ tsp baking powder
½ tsp bicarbonate of soda
½ tsp sea salt
75ml vegan milk (I used almond)
300g vegan chocolate, chopped

Line 2–3 large baking trays with parchment paper.

In a large bowl, beat the vegan butter, sugar and vanilla extract together until combined. Add the flour, baking powder, bicarbonate of soda and sea salt and beat again until combined. Gradually add the vegan milk until you have a cookie dough. Fold through the chopped vegan chocolate. Divide the cookie dough into pieces about 80g each, and place onto the lined trays. Chill in the fridge for 1 hour or freeze for 30 minutes.

Preheat the oven to 200°C/180°C fan.

Once the cookies have chilled, bake in the oven for 10–11 minutes. Leave to cool fully on the trays.

VEGAN VICTORIA SPONGE

A delightfully light and fluffy two-layer vegan Victoria sponge, sandwiched with a vanilla buttercream frosting, jam and decorated with strawberries... what more could you want?! This vegan sponge is so delicate but light, and I am so proud of this recipe. It creates a beautiful base if you need a vegan sponge alternative – chill the sponge before decorating and it'll be a dream. You can even make it chocolate flavoured by substituting 50g of flour for cocoa powder.

SERVES: 12+

PREP: 20 minutes
BAKE: 35–45 minutes
COOL: 1 hour
DECORATE: 30 minutes
LASTS: 3+ days, at
room temperature

450g self-raising flour
150g soft light brown sugar
150g caster sugar
1 tsp baking powder
1 tsp bicarbonate of soda
400ml vegan milk (I use almond)
175ml vegetable oil
2 tsp vanilla extract
1 tbsp white wine vinegar

Decoration

150g vegan butter
350g icing sugar
1 tsp vanilla extract
200g jam of your choice
12 whole strawberries

Preheat the oven to 180°C/160°C fan and line two 20cm cake tins with parchment paper.

In a large bowl, mix the flour, brown sugar, caster sugar, baking powder and bicarbonate of soda together until combined. Add the vegan milk, vegetable oil, vanilla extract and white wine vinegar and stir until combined. Divide the mixture between the two tins. Bake in the oven for 35–45 minutes. Leave to cool fully in the tins.

Decoration

In a large bowl, beat the vegan butter to soften it. Add the icing sugar and vanilla extract and beat until combined. Grab the first sponge and spread half of the buttercream onto the cake. Spread the jam over the top. Top with the other sponge and spread the rest of the buttercream over the top. Decorate with the strawberries.

VEGAN VANILLA CHEESECAKE

This cheesecake is creamy, packed full of beautiful vanilla flavour and is a beautiful base recipe for a vegan treat. Using full-fat ingredients and being patient during the setting time are the two simple rules for all cheesecakes, vegan or not. This cheesecake is INCREDIBLY easy to make, and you can adapt and change it as you prefer. Fold 200g vegan melted chocolate through the mix before pouring into the tin and you'll have a chocolate version!

SERVES: 12

PREP: 20 minutes
SET: 5–6 hours
DECORATE: 20 minutes
LASTS: 3 days,
in the fridge

300g digestive biscuits
100g vegan butter, melted

Cheesecake

500g vegan soft cheese
75g icing sugar
2 tsp vanilla extract
250ml vegan double cream or
    coconut cream
Fruit coulis
Fruit (I used 12 whole strawberries)

Blitz the biscuits to a fine crumb in a food processor or crush in a bowl with a rolling pin.

Add the melted vegan butter and mix together. Press into the base of a 20cm springform cake tin.

Cheesecake

In a large bowl, mix the vegan soft cheese, icing sugar and vanilla extract together until combined. In a separate bowl, whip the vegan cream until stiff peaks form. Fold the two mixtures together. Spread over the biscuit base and set in the fridge for 5–6 hours. Decorate with a fruit coulis, fruit, or whatever you fancy.

GLUTEN-FREE BROWNIES

These brownies are super chocolatey, super fudgy and I adore them. A simple swap to gluten-free flour brings you something utterly spectacular. I always add chocolate chips to my brownies and you can use any flavour you fancy. You can even flavour your brownies with 1 teaspoon of flavouring of your choice. Setting them in the fridge is a top tip for the fudgiest of brownies.

MAKES: 16

PREP: 20 minutes
BAKE: 25–30 minutes
COOL: 2 hours
SET: 3 hours
LASTS: 4+ days, at room temperature

200g dark chocolate
200g unsalted butter
4 eggs
275g caster sugar
50g cocoa powder
100g gluten-free plain flour
300g chocolate chips of your choice

Preheat the oven to 180°C/160°C fan and line a 23cm square baking tin with parchment paper.

In a heatproof bowl, break up the dark chocolate into pieces and add the butter. Melt together in the microwave in short bursts or set the bowl over a pan of simmering water (bain-marie) until smooth. Leave to cool.

Add the eggs and sugar to a bowl and whisk until mousse-like and doubled in size. Pour over the cooled chocolate mixture and fold together carefully. Add the cocoa powder and flour and then gently fold together again. Fold through the chocolate chips and pour into the tin.

Bake in the oven for 25–30 minutes. Leave to cool completely in the tin, then chill in the fridge for a few hours for best results. Cut into squares with a sharp knife and enjoy.

GLUTEN-FREE CUPCAKES

Deliciously moist and fluffy gluten-free vanilla cupcakes with a vanilla buttercream frosting – a delicious base recipe for so many bakes! These beauties are so easy to throw together and make the best basic gluten-free cupcake recipe. You can decorate them how you fancy using this recipe as inspiration. Have fun!

MAKES: 12

PREP: 20 minutes
BAKE: 20–22 minutes
COOL: 1 hour
DECORATE: 30 minutes
LASTS: 3+ days, at
room temperature

200g unsalted butter, at room
 temperature
200g caster sugar
200g gluten-free self-raising flour
4 eggs
¼ tsp xanthan gum
1 tsp vanilla extract

Decoration

200g unsalted butter, at room
 temperature
400g icing sugar
1 tsp vanilla extract
Gluten-free sprinkles

Preheat the oven to 180°C/160°C fan and put 12 cupcake or muffin cases on a baking tray.

In a large bowl, beat the butter and sugar together until light and fluffy. Add the flour, eggs, xanthan gum and vanilla extract and beat together until smooth. Divide between the 12 cases and bake in the oven for 20–22 minutes. Leave to cool fully.

Decoration

In a large bowl, beat the butter for a few minutes to soften it. Add the icing sugar and vanilla extract and beat until smooth. Transfer to a piping bag with the piping nozzle of your choice fitted and pipe onto the cupcakes however you fancy. Decorate with some gluten-free sprinkles.

GLUTEN-FREE BREAD

So how about making a deliciously soft gluten-free bread that is a beautiful base for toasties, sandwiches, or even to dip into soup? It's super simple, and I love it. It has a light texture from the plain flour, but the xanthan gum brings it together to create a wonderful bread. Feel free to add some seeds (up to 100g) for a textured loaf.

MAKES: 1 loaf

PREP: 45 minutes
BAKE: 55–60 minutes
COOL: 1 hour
LASTS: Best served fresh

350g gluten-free plain flour, plus extra for dusting
15g caster sugar
12g dried active yeast
2 tsp xanthan gum
3 tsp baking powder
Pinch of salt
1 egg
35ml olive oil, plus extra for greasing
350ml warm water

Grease and flour a 900g loaf tin.

In a large bowl, mix the flour, sugar, yeast, xanthan gum, baking powder and salt together to combine. Add the egg, olive oil and warm water and knead the mixture for a few minutes to combine. Place the loaf in the tin, cover and leave to rise in a warm place for about 30 minutes.

Preheat the oven to 200°C/180°C fan.

Bake in the oven for 55–60 minutes. Check that it's ready by turning out the loaf and tapping the bottom – it should make a hollow sound. Leave to cool fully on a wire rack.

Conversion Table

Weights *

METRIC	IMPERIAL
15 g	½ oz
25 g	1 oz
40 g	1½ oz
50 g	2 oz
75 g	3 oz
100 g	4 oz
150 g	5 oz
175 g	6 oz
200 g	7 oz
225 g	8 oz
250 g	9 oz
275 g	10 oz
350 g	12 oz
375 g	13 oz
400 g	14 oz
425 g	15 oz
450 g	1 lb
550 g	1¼ lb
675 g	1½ lb
900 g	2 lb
1.5 kg	3 lb
1.75 kg	4 lb
2.25 kg	5 lb

*28.35g = 1oz but the measurements here have been rounded up or down to make conversion easier

Volume

METRIC	IMPERIAL
25 ml	1 fl oz
50 ml	2 fl oz
85 ml	3 fl oz
150 ml	5 fl oz (¼ pint)
300 ml	10 fl oz (¼ pint)
450 ml	15 fl oz (¾ pint)
600 ml	1 pint
700 ml	1¼ pints
900 ml	1½ pints
1 litres	1¾ pints
1.2 litres	2 pints
1.25 litres	2¼ pints
1.5 litres	2½ pints
1.6 litres	2¾ pints
1.75 litres	3 pints
1.8 litres	3¼ pints
2 litres	3½ pints
2.1 litres	3¾ pints
2.25 litres	4 pints
2.75 litres	5 pints
3.4 litres	6 pints
3.9 litres	7 pints
5 litres	8 pints (1 gal)

Measurements

METRIC	IMPERIAL
0.5 cm	¼ inch
1 cm	½ inch
2.5 cm	1 inch
5 cm	2 inches
7.5 cm	3 inches
10 cm	4 inches
15 cm	6 inches
18 cm	7 inches
20 cm	8 inches
23 cm	9 inches
25 cm	10 inches
30 cm	12 inches

Oven Temperatures

140°C	275°F	Gas Mk 1
150°C	300°F	Gas Mk 2
160°C	325°F	Gas Mk 3
180°C	350°F	Gas Mk 4
190°C	375°F	Gas Mk 5
200°C	400°F	Gas Mk 6
220°C	425°F	Gas Mk 7
230°C	450°F	Gas Mk 8
240°C	475°F	Gas Mk 9

Index

Acknowledgments

My Mum

We may not like to admit it, but we are really similar. I have witnessed you working SO hard throughout your life, and even in retirement you are still working and doing everything you can to help support the family. I take more inspiration from you than I am probably willing to admit, because I admire you so much. You motivate me to do the same in my life, and I know that I will look after my future family in the same way.

My Dad

Whenever something in my house is broken and I haven't got a clue how to fix it, you are straight there. If I have a delivery for anything work related, you jump at the chance to help - and it may sound silly and simple, but it really is the biggest help on the planet. It's been a hard few years for you, but I know you are so proud of me and I can't thank you enough.

My Brother

Thank you for always being there for me, especially when I need someone to look after the cats. My aim in life is that we will always be close, and that we continue to grow together. I always want to be there for you, as I know you always will be for me.

My Friends

You accept me for who I am, you trust me, and you support me always. You have all seen me at the lowest of lows and helped me get through it all to be where I am now - I honestly adore you all. Whether it's going for walks at 7am on a Sunday winter morning to get a breath of fresh air, having a glass of wine and listening to me rant about drama in my life, testing my recipes and giving me honest feedback, you are all there for me and you are special.

You have all known me since before my world of baking started, and I am so happy that you are still here, supporting me along the way, and being the best cheerleaders a girl could ask for. I hope you all know that I will never be able to say thank you enough.

Sam, Alice & Abby

I think all three of you know how much I appreciate you. You guys have by far been the best team I could have asked for... and here we are, on book THREE!! This is absolute madness. Thank you for continuously having the confidence in me and my world.

Sam

You are the editor of dreams. You know my brain so well, and you know what will work. You understand me and what I want to achieve, and you help me bring that to life.

Alice

You help me grow in confidence in so many ways with the things I have done now to help promote my books and world, and I cannot thank you enough - I also love the coffees and snacks we have on these adventures.

Abby

You have all the knowledge in the world to help my book grow to be what it should be and what to do with it all, I wouldn't have a clue with where to start

and you have made it all possible. I am forever thankful.

Ellis

You know how much I adore you and your photography skills, but you are also just one of the kindest and loveliest humans I've ever met. I have never felt more comfortable with someone, considering how much I hate photos of myself, and you do it every time! You have an unbelievable skill, and you are pure magic when it comes to photographing my recipes, and I couldn't have had anyone better help me bring my books to life. The first thing people look for in a recipe is the photo, and your photos so perfectly show my ideas.

Sarah, Max & Co

The fact that you all so lovingly and perfectly brought my book to life is just insane… it's magical, it's perfect, and it is an absolute vision. The props are a dream, and they suit the bakes and book so well - and I wanted to steal them all. My recipes being baked and cooked so perfectly, as always, is the most important part. Visually seeing something so delicious and inviting is what makes people want to make the recipes, and you all do it so well. I have complete trust in you to make my recipes beautiful.

And most importantly, to my followers...

You are the people who made this all happen. You are the people who let me have THREE BOOKS?! You have all helped me have opportunities that I never thought were possible: baking on live tv, baking in front of thousands of people on stage, having the fastest selling baking book ever, and the chance to turn my hobby and passion into a career of a lifetime. I honestly cannot say thank you enough, but without you none of this would be possible.

I have always wanted to make sure that I give you the recipes that you want, as getting the chance to experiment with ideas that give you joy is an unbeatable experience. My happiness is overwhelming when I see people across the world enjoying something that I had fun creating, whether it's a quick bake like cookies, someone's birthday cake, or a meal they want to cook for the family. Baking and cooking is something people can relate to all over the world, and it brings everyone together, and I hope you all adore this book for that as well.

To my younger self

If you ever think you aren't good enough, you are wrong. No matter what you want to do in life, follow your passions and do what you want to do because you only get one chance at life, and you deserve to be happy. I spent years of my life hiding away from what I wanted to do and loved doing, and for what? Taking the leap into this world has changed my life, and I am so glad that at one point my younger self told me to take that leap.

Jane x

4

Published in 2023 by Ebury Press an imprint of Ebury Publishing,

20 Vauxhall Bridge Road,
London SW1V 2SA

Ebury Press is part of the Penguin Random House group of companies
whose addresses can be found at global.penguinrandomhouse.com

Text © Jane Dunn 2023
Photography © Ellis Parrinder 2023

Jane Dunn has asserted her right to be identified as the author of this
Work in accordance with the Copyright, Designs and Patents Act 1988

First published by Ebury Press in 2023

www.penguin.co.uk

A CIP catalogue record for this book is available from the British Library

ISBN 9781529196818

Design: Studio Nic & Lou
Photography: Ellis Parrinder
Food Styling: Sarah Hardy
Prop Styling: Max Robinson

Printed and bound in Great Britain by Bell and Bain Ltd, Glasgow

The authorised representative in the EEA is Penguin Random House Ireland, Morrison Chambers,
32 Nassau Street, Dublin D02 YH68.

Penguin Random House is committed to a sustainable future for our business, our readers and our
planet. This book is made from Forest Stewardship Council® certified paper.